Praise for *Average at Best*

'We all knew she had the music in her. Who knew she had the words? All these beautiful, hilarious, heart-stealing, soul-filling words!

This is pure book gold from a rare and glistening national treasure. The raw and wild story behind a global phenomenon – and the best three hours I've ever spent inside a pub! The story of an anything-but-average woman who dared to open up her sound hole and let her dreams fly across the world.'
Trent Dalton, author of *Boy Swallows Universe*

'Millions of people who've attended and watched Pub Choir already know the unmatched electricity that Astrid Jorgensen generates when she conducts. Turns out, she's just as electric on the page. Hilarious and infectiously giddy, this behind-the-scenes look at a global phenomenon is a companion for life, nothing short of a superhero origin story and contains the most triumphant story involving poo that I've ever read.'
Benjamin Law, writer and broadcaster

'On stage, Astrid Jorgensen transforms from introverted music nerd into a choral colossus. In these pages, she is revealed as a beautiful writer who blends heart, wit and insight with rare skill.'
Andrew McMillen, author and national music writer at *The Australian*

'Astrid is a force of nature. But never has there been a more inappropriately titled memoir. There's nothing average about Astrid Jorgensen. Her memoir is testament to the fact she's a mix of magic, mayhem and sheer brilliance. I loved every line. For anyone who's ever been curious about the phenomenon that is Pub Choir and the crazy woman waving her arms around at the front of the stage – read this book.'
Bec Sparrow, writer, podcaster and co-founder of Birds of a Feather Book Club

'Astrid Jorgensen is a national treasure – funny, captivating, and wildly talented. Part maestro, part comedian, she's transformed group singing into a joyous, unforgettable experience that makes everyone feel like they belong.'
Sally Hepworth, author of *The Good Sister*

'Take a joy-filled road trip with Astrid in her Daewoo Matiz, via a nunnery, a few false starts, and some excellent side quests all the way to where she teaches the world to sing.

Average at Best is anything but. A sharply observed, at times hilarious and poignant debut. You hold in your hands a book about the joy of letting go.'
Frances Whiting, award-winning journalist, columnist and author

'I have stood in the crowd at Pub Choir as an audience member and been entranced by Astrid's ability to make a room feel like a single organism. I have stood on stage next to Astrid and experienced the waves of love, trust and joy that flows back at her in gratitude. And now I have read her words, experiencing music through her eyes, and falling in love with my own chosen medium in ways I didn't know were possible.

Astrid Jorgensen is a national treasure.'
Ben Lee, Australian musician and actor

'Astrid Jorgensen turns language into lyrics and stories into symphonies. Bewitchingly brilliant and wildly original. This book sings.'
Lise Carlaw and Sarah Wills, podcasters and founders of DISCO CLUB

AVERAGE AT BEST

AVERAGE AT BEST

PUB CHOIR'S
ASTRID JORGENSEN

Astrid

SIMON & SCHUSTER

New York • Amsterdam/Antwerp • London • Toronto • Sydney/Melbourne • New Delhi

AVERAGE AT BEST: A MEMOIR FROM THE CREATOR OF PUB CHOIR®
First published in Australia in 2025 by
Simon & Schuster (Australia) Pty Limited
Level 4, 32 York St, Sydney NSW 2000

10 9 8 7 6 5 4 3 2 1

New York Amsterdam/Antwerp London Toronto Sydney/Melbourne New Delhi
Visit our website at www.simonandschuster.com.au

For more than 100 years, Simon & Schuster has championed authors and the stories they create. By respecting the copyright of an author's intellectual property, you enable Simon & Schuster and the author to continue publishing exceptional books for years to come. We thank you for supporting the author's copyright by purchasing an authorised edition of this book.

No amount of this book may be reproduced or stored in any format, nor may it be uploaded to any website, database, language-learning model, or other repository, retrieval, or artificial intelligence system without express permission. All rights reserved. Inquiries may be directed to Simon & Schuster, 1230 Avenue of the Americas, New York, NY 10020 or permissions@simonandschuster.com.

© Astrid Jorgensen 2025

All rights reserved. No part of this publication may be reproduced, stored in a retrieval system, or transmitted in any form or by any means, electronic, mechanical, photocopying, recording or otherwise, without prior permission of the publisher.

A catalogue record for this book is available from the National Library of Australia

ISBN: 9781761634208

Cover design: George Saad
Back cover image: Jacob Morrison
Typeset by Midland Typesetters, Australia
Printed and bound by CPI Group (UK) Ltd, Croydon CR0 4YY

Pub Choir® is a registered trade mark of Astrid Jorgensen.

The authorised representative in the EEA is Simon & Schuster Netherlands BV, Herculesplein 96, 3584 AA Utrecht, Netherlands. info@simonandschuster.nl

*for Little Astrid
and for June*

CONTENTS

Foreword	xi
Introduction	1
Altar Ego	5
Misophonia	19
Alter Ego	25
Lesson Plan	35
It's All Relative	47
Steady Hands	61
And I Am Strong	65
Fuck Around and Find Out	77
Jaw-Dropping	91
Mansplaining	103
The Event Horizon	117
Lost in Translation	127

It's Complimentary	139
15 Reasons I Might Not Sleep Tonight	151
Old Dog, New Tricks	159
Pivot	175
Gossip Girl	187
The Elephant in the Room	193
Don't Shit in Glass Houses	207
June	221
Acknowledgements	233
About the author	237

FOREWORD
ELLA HOOPER

While singing together is the great unifier, singing in public is the great terrifier!

It's a rare wizard who has the sleight of hand required to prevent a group of people from immolating in a fire of their own self-critique.

But Astrid can do it.

I've seen it with my own eyes. From being onstage as a Pub Choir guest to being an audience member when I once slipped in to experience the crowd-feel incognito.

I've been a professional singer going on twenty-five years. You'd think I would have chilled out about my job by now. But singing is one of those things, like self-image, where lots of highly personal triggers and traps lie in wait. If I'm not careful, I can start feeling self-conscious or even competitive – about something that was never meant to be a competition.

As our culture has drifted away from community towards the cult of the individual, expressing ourselves collectively has become diluted in a sea of online tippy-tappy. Comments and likes have replaced actual human connections and vibrational experiences.

We need to get back into our bodies! We need to sing! The high you get when singing in harmony with others, with those self-generated soundwaves travelling through your skull – your entire body – is like nothing else.

If you were raised a little bit hippy (like me) or a little bit religious (like Astrid), maybe you were lucky enough to get a dose of the good stuff young. But no one is immune to living in the modern world, which shrinks and shrivels our confidence.

Being swept up in a shared moment of creativity, feeling that vital release – even shedding a tear or two – is our collective birthright. Gosh, singing together might just save the world. And even though she didn't actually become a nun (lucky for us), I don't think it's too bombastic to say that Astrid, through Pub Choir, is doing God's work.

Astrid and I might come from a similar star system, because we're both passionate about unsubscribing from that stuffy ideal of perfectionism. That unattainable pedestal that elevates us to even more self-doubt. This book is an exploration of how she came to be a committed pedestal dismantler.

My band, Killing Heidi, sent a similar message to other teenage girls and various weirdos – that it's okay and *normal* to be and feel imperfect. Perfect doesn't exist, and pursuing that false state can really harm you. Let yourself off the hook,

FOREWORD

let your hair down or (in my case) let it knot up so completely that it becomes a now-questionable, but at the same time wonderfully outré, hairstyle.

Astrid claims that this is not a self-help book, but in reading it, my self felt helped. I laughed; I felt lifted, heart-punched and activated; and I nearly gave myself a crick in the neck nodding furiously in recognition throughout these chapters. I felt seen. I felt allowed. I felt like I was back in the audience at Pub Choir.

Astrid is an uber-talented choirmaster, yes. A wholesome, piss-funny comedienne, yes. But she's something else on top of all that. What do you call a 'safe space creator'? A social shaman? A heart alchemist? Maybe we just call this magic 'Astrid'.

Ella Hooper | singer and songwriter

INTRODUCTION

My first car was a glorified sheet of aluminium foil called a Daewoo Matiz. I was nineteen years old and couldn't afford to buy a car, so I was ecstatic when Phillip, one of my older brothers, bequeathed it to me when he left Australia to study abroad. He'd been driving it for a few years and told me to take care of it. I felt an incredible freedom sitting in this tiny metallic bubble, even though the whole vehicle wobbled from the breeze of any passing truck, motorbike or pedestrian. Not having to catch two buses to get to work made me feel invincible.

I loved driving that piece of shit.

I also can't believe I lived to write this book.

One time behind the wheel, I felt some kind of strange, gentle tapping near my feet. At the next red light, I looked down by the foot pedals and saw that my shoes were sprinkled with some sort of black, plasticky substance. *What the hell is that?* I kept driving. At the next set of lights, even more of this mysterious stuff had appeared. It was now covering the footwell. *Where was it all coming from?* I was nearly home; I'd investigate when I got there.

As I turned the last corner onto my street, the steering wheel came away in my hands. The steering column had disintegrated and was crumbling to bits while I drove. I coasted up to my driveway and felt like I'd won a Grand Prix.

Would you believe that this was not the final straw for the Matiz? I called a mechanic, who towed this Christmas-cracker-quality car and replaced its steering column and steering wheel. I don't know much about cars, but I know you need those bits.

This cute little manual (stick-shift) deathtrap sprayed toxic gas through the air-conditioning vents, couldn't drive the speed limit on motorways, and you could forget about taking a passenger if there was an incline involved on the journey. But it wasn't until the gearstick broke off in my hand while driving that I decided it was over. I happened to be in second gear, which is your best option if your gearstick snaps. Once again, I was magically close to home. So I put on my hazard lights, revved slowly to my destination and re-evaluated my life.

In this book, you won't learn anything about self-help or how to win all the time. This is a memoir about embracing the mediocrity of life. I hope you don't think my writing is mediocre (but if you do, the book is called *Average at Best* so the clue was right there on the cover). But the title isn't really a disclaimer about my literary proficiency, it's how

INTRODUCTION

I view myself as a person. But also how I view you (rude), and everybody who has ever lived. I honestly believe we are all average at best.

I mean, sure. Some people are verifiably the best at certain things. Maybe you're one of them – congratulations! Somebody can run 100 metres faster than all other people on the planet. Some woman has the world record for eating more hotdogs than anybody else in one minute. But *so what?* (Both of those feats are impressive, by the way!) Being the best at something *is* an achievement worth celebrating. But what about every other part of your life?

The odds are, at almost every moment, you're not the best *or* the worst at whatever it is you're doing. There are billions of people on earth. It's far more likely that your actions will fall somewhere in the vastness between 'best' and 'worst'. That's where most of life is lived – in the all-encompassing, electrifying average of everything else. I'm not trying to bum you out, I honestly think it's very freeing to stop striving for 'best' all the time. By its very nature, 'best' is rare and elusive; you're not going to get much of it in life. And I sure don't want to miss out on deeply experiencing the fullness of my one precious existence by searching for the sliver of 'best'.

I am probably not the best at anything. When I'm onstage performing at my show Pub Choir, I *believe* I'm the best in the world at delivering improvised comedy choir lessons to large groups of musically untrained strangers. But there is no way to verify this. When it comes to music, art, comedy or any kind of performance, there is no 'best'. We can only try our best and maybe, in the process, feel better.

This is a book about all the ways I've tried my best to feel better. I promise, it's not sickly sweet and positive. I tell the truth (probably too much). Some of my stories are about the times I won. But more often, I'm metaphorically back in the Matiz, with no gearstick, no steering wheel and no fucking clue – simply relieved if I manage to safely coast home.

Thank you for picking up this book. I'm humbled that you're considering reading it.

ALTAR EGO

When I was sixteen years old, I flew alone to Zambia to live in a convent and become a Catholic nun.

Anybody who has attended my foul-mouthed and chaotic show, Pub Choir, might find this a bit of a surprise, so let me start by saying that, at the time of writing this in 2025, I'm a nasty little unbeliever who is gleefully living in sin. But in 2006, I wanted to marry Jesus, and Zambia's capital Lusaka was to be the backdrop of our romance.

I didn't tell my parents about my holy ambitions when booking the flights. I simply expressed that, to celebrate graduating high school, I wished to spend the money I'd earned working at the local bakery by visiting my Aunt Jacinta. She had been living and working in Zambia for twenty-odd years. She also just happens to be a nun. To be more precise, she is a Franciscan Missionary of the Divine Motherhood (FMDM on the streets). I campaigned to my parents, 'How much mischief could I *really* get up to, holidaying with a nun for two months when I finish school?' Those chumps agreed to let me go.

My Zambian adventure also raised the eyebrows of a few schoolfriends. To get them off my case, I loudly talked up my trip like it would be as edgy and cool as *their* graduation parties. Sure, *they* would be raving on a beach drinking vodka with handsy boys, but *I* would be on a safari (at a church service) meeting cute boys of my own (listening to old priests) and taking edibles (communion wafers).

It was a relief to have an excuse to skip the graduation afterparties. I felt too young and naïve to attend (but old enough to marry Jesus, go figure!). I was a full year younger than everybody else in my grade because I'd started school earlier than recommended. I'm not humble bragging – this was not a decision based on merit. With four very clever older brothers, who all attended school at the suggested age, my parents are unable to articulate what happened with me; that is, I'm pretty sure they briefly forgot what year I was born.

Maybe you think I've hammed up this story for a book, so I will submit the following as further evidence: my family celebrated my birthday on the wrong day for five years until I glimpsed my birth certificate and fact-checked it with my parents.

'Mum, my birth certificate is wrong!'

'What do you mean?'

'Well, it says I was born on April 22nd, but my birthday is on April 23rd . . . isn't it?'

There was a thoughtful silence as my parents looked at each other, eyebrows raised.

'Huh,' said Dad, 'would you look at that? April 22nd does ring a bell, now you mention it.'

I truly have no hard feelings over this. Five children is *a lot* of children. I imagine that, by the tail end of the litter, the placental timelines get a bit murky. I'm not trying to elicit pity, but demonstrate that being the youngest of five children means that your parents are very experienced but also very tired. And if you don't sweat the small stuff, like your date of birth, you can fly under the radar and do some fairly outrageous shit. Such as travelling to Zambia by yourself for two months when you're sixteen with only $400 in small change.

In true 'youngest child' fashion, I did very little to prepare for my trip. I've never been one to worry about my personal safety, and given I was flying around the world to double-check I could take a vow of poverty, 400 bucks felt like more than enough. My only real worry was that I wouldn't recognise my aunty when I arrived in Zambia.

We'd only met once before, when I was ten, at a family reunion in Singapore. I was quietly obsessed with her. She was my mum's literal sister, but simultaneously everybody's. I'd always wanted a sister and here she was: Sister Jacinta! She was friendly and chatty and clearly unbothered by the latest fashions and fads – every day, she wore the same simple beige clothes and a stiff-looking habit to cover her hair. I thought it made her look unbelievably cool. And I was transfixed by her face. Sister Jacinta had smooth olive skin with gentle freckles and a wide, square jawline. As in, she looked exactly like my mum, except . . . *peaceful* (possibly something to do with not having to raise five yappy children who were relentlessly pinching each other).

At some point during the reunion, I plucked up the courage to ask, 'Sister Jacinta, when did you know you wanted to be a nun?'

She serenely replied, 'Wán pí [her affectionate nickname for me, meaning 'naughty/cheeky'], I heard the voice of God calling me to this life.' God's voice was quiet at first, she told me, but the more she listened, the louder and more insistent it became until she couldn't ignore it anymore.

I listened to her with awe. I wanted to be like my aunty. I wanted to have a daily outfit. I wanted to be nice to people and to do good things in the world. And I *especially* wanted God to speak to me. Quietly.

Growing up in a family of seven, somebody was always hollering about *something* at home. We had an actual cow bell to announce that dinner was ready. Whoever was closest at that moment would clang the bell while helpfully yelling, 'DINNER'S READY.' No shit! If somebody needed a message delivered, we'd *never* physically go to them; instead, we'd remain in our place and shout:

'HUGH, THE GIRL YOU LIKE IS ON THE PHONE. WHAT DO YOU WANT ME TO TELL HER? SHOULD I PRETEND YOU AREN'T HOME?'

Mum was always blending or juicing some heavy-duty health potion in the kitchen made of carrots and what sounded like spoons. Somebody was always stomping on the floorboards wearing wooden clogs (also Mum). For goodness' sake, my brother Malcolm even played the bagpipes. He's deaf in his right ear but I've always believed he knew what he was inflicting upon us in surround sound. I tell you: our house was *noisy*.

What if God had been whispering messages to me this whole time, and I'd missed them for all the bloody racket?

At night, I began closing the door to my bedroom. I use the term 'bedroom' loosely – I slept in a repurposed greenhouse at the front of the family home. Every single wall was made of glass and the temperature inside was incompatible with human life during sunlight hours. I'd close the curtains so my brothers couldn't see me being extremely weird, then I'd kneel down and cover my ears to block out as much noise as I could.

I listened. I strained. I heaved. But I couldn't hear God at all.

What about a sign? Maybe God had changed contact methods? 'If you want me to be a nun, flicker my bedroom lights!' *Nothing.* 'If I should be a nun, make the TV turn on!' *Silence.* I narrowed my eyes at an electrical outlet and tried to make it short-circuit with my mind. Had I confused the mystery of God with Roald Dahl's *Matilda*? Being unable to start a single electrical fire confirmed my suspicions that my aunty was chosen and special, but I was not. God had spoken directly to her, but wouldn't even lightly haunt the electrics in my room.

What I didn't yet realise is that I have no 'inner monologue'. That most people can apparently hear voices speaking in their mind, like a narration of their thoughts, is completely foreign to me. I can't hear a word. I can remember conversations I've had, but I can't replay them as a soundtrack, nor can I rehearse future conversations in my head. My thoughts are wordless concepts and urges.

I can't visualise anything in my mind's eye, either. If I close my eyes, I . . . can't see anymore? I can't picture anyone's face, or an apple; all I can see is the inside of my eyelids.

I've since learned that the absence of mental imagery is called 'aphantasia', but when I was ten I had no idea how other people thought. I had no idea about anything, really. Which is why it was so phenomenal to me when I finally heard *a voice in my brain.*

When it happened, I was once again kneeling on the tiles of my hothouse, ears covered, staring at a small, plastic, bedside figurine of my future mother-in-law, Mary. 'Speak to me, Mary. Speak to me, God. Just say if you want me to become a nun like my aunty,' I incanted under my breath. 'Say something. Say SOMETHING!'

'Astriiiiiid . . .' came a wheezy reply inside my brain. 'You . . . should be . . . A NUN.'

A straightforward message delivered in an asthmatic way. It was weird how God's voice sounded exactly like *my* voice, but surely that was just God making a clever point.

It was so rare and unusual to 'hear' specific words in my brain, I truly thought I was having a spiritual revelation. In reality, I had experienced A *Thought*. Like people have sometimes. I had wished and willed God to speak to me for so long that my suggestible, arid mind finally squeezed out this miniscule audio crumb and I gobbled it up like manna from heaven. I never heard God's voice again, but once was enough for me. I felt chosen (which is not something fifth children say very often).

Armed with my heavenly DM, I focused all my attention on marrying the most famous nepo-baby in history: the Son of God.

On Christmas Day 2006, I boarded the plane to Lusaka, wearing flip-flops and holding a bag packed with just two pairs of brown pants and two T-shirts. The aircraft was almost empty.

The flight attendants tried doting on me, to no avail. 'Are you *sure* you don't want an extra meal? A little chocolate for later?' they probed.

'Oh no,' I fatly whispered, 'I don't need anything, I'm not hungry.' I imagined them returning to the galley, all agreeing that 'She's the best passenger we've ever had', and 'Her self-control is so impressive, it's almost like she's taken some vow of poverty.'

At the airport, I recognised my aunty instantly (what a relief), and off we went to the FMDM house in Lusaka. There, everything I knew about convent life – learned from my rigorous study of the movie *Sister Act* starring Whoopi

Goldberg – seemed to be real. These softly spoken, cloistered women sang, ate, worked and prayed together up to five times daily. Every chore was tended to with care, and every surface was spotless. (Which is so much easier to achieve when your four grotty teenage brothers don't live in the same house.)

The FMDM sisters let me tag along and gawk at everything they did. I followed the nuns who were qualified teachers into local schools to 'assist' with their lessons.

'What's the tallest mountain in Australia? Oh . . . Mount . . . Gravatt, I think.' (The pre-internet days were incredible for telling lies.)

I shadowed those who were nurses into community hospices and 'helped' clean wounds and pretended I wasn't at all bothered.

'Who, *me*? Oh no, I don't mind the smell of that lanced boil, not a bit!' I trilled with a panicky smile on my face, while swallowing the little bit of sick at the back of my throat.

While scraping the tumour-ridden, pus-caked groin of a man suffering horrifically through the end stages of AIDS, it did flicker across my mind that, perhaps, nunhood was a bit too hardcore for me. But any unpleasantness during the day was *more* than balanced by the satisfaction that coursed through me as I experienced unrivalled quiet inside the convent walls.

For the first time in my life, everybody *shut up*. On New Year's Eve, the FMDM sisters imposed a Great Silence for the hours leading up to midnight, while sitting together and praying for the world. Of course, given that I can't conjure any specific words in my mind, I just sat on my cushion for several hours, doing and saying nothing, in a blank state of total ecstasy. *Finally,* a bit of shush.

In a time just before the world adopted a permanent state of online connectivity, I barely contacted home for two months. I felt like I had the chance to try on a new personality and properly test-drive the nun lifestyle. I could pretend I was the sort of person who had *always* used the sun to mark my sleep schedule. Nobody needed to know that I usually spent school holidays awake until 2 am, torturing my Sims on the family computer, and desperately hoping I wouldn't get caught watching late-night international films for the full-frontal nudity. That was unless I had a shift at the bakery, where I would spend the day gorging myself on stolen croissants, my pockets filled with loose change that never made it to the till.

The FMDM sisters were gently responding to a sincere calling to humility, service and faith. But sixteen-year-old me was too young and idiotic to understand that becoming a nun for the lifestyle benefits and social detox was ill-advised and offensive *at best*. On top of this, a big red flag was waving right in front of my face, which I pretended not to notice (easy if I closed my eyes). When I tagged along to the many daily prayer sessions, I simply wasn't thinking about my boyfriend Jesus.

The moment I flip-flopped my feet through the door of my first Zambian church service, my relationship with Him was in big trouble. No matter how many Hail Marys I muttered, or how firmly I clasped my hands to pray, I couldn't concentrate on *anything* except the singing. I wanted to love Jesus, who just like me wore opened-toed shoes in formal settings. But the music was just *too good*. Too distracting. It was an unexpected love triangle – a most unholy trinity.

As a child, I received consistent piano and violin lessons. I taught myself to play the guitar, bassoon and trombone to a passable level. I frequently sang at school events, and I'd just topped all the music subjects in my senior year. Yet up to five times a day I would follow the sisters into prayer and be musically *destroyed* by everyone around me.

When the jangly guitars and egg shakers kicked off the next hymn, everybody in the church unleashed flawless vocal harmonies while stylishly dancing to – what seemed to me – a different song from the one we were singing. I tried desperately to make sense of what was happening. *I think . . . this song is in 4/4 time? No. Maybe it's 3/4 time? . . . Wait! Why is everybody dancing in 13/5? Is that toddler clapping in polyrhythms of seven? Did that woman just take a tambourine out of her purse?* I felt immobilised. I didn't know what to do with my hands, when to sing or where to look. I was outclassed and out-musicked at every turn.

Being so musically inferior in this setting had an extra sting to it. Just before I left for my holy pilgrimage, I'd found out that I didn't pass my audition to study music at university. Me! The top music student at my school! The best musician I'd ever met! The cruel injustice of being denied entry into the opera course, even though I'd flawlessly performed a song from *Phantom of the Opera* for my audition. It literally had 'opera' in the title, hello? What more could *anybody* have possibly done?

Now, I had flown around the world to once again find myself singing from the wrong songbook. And yet, it felt *amazing*. Unable to contribute, I was simply submerged in a feeling. The music wasn't a performance for anybody; it was a shared, hopeful experience. I had never witnessed anything so beautiful or collaborative. Simultaneously, nobody and everybody was in charge. I was wildly swivelling my head to take it all in, but every other person in the room was lost in the moment, offering up their unique voice to each other and beyond.

All too soon, my *Sister Act* movie montage was at an end. My aunty bundled me onto the plane back to Australia and I felt transcendent and brand new. I decided that I was *definitely* going to become a nun . . . as soon as I had the courage to tell other people. I squirrelled away my holy secret and tried to build up the nerve to announce my love for the Lord. But the words wouldn't come out of my mouth.

Desperate for validation, I decided to contact some local nuns. I looked up where the FMDM sisters lived in Australia, and found a chapter in Bendigo. I wrote to them, begging to join their ranks. In return, I received the kindest rejection letter of my life, which included the following advice from a Sister Monica:

It is exciting that the presence of God is so strong in your life – what a wonderful gift. However, it would be very wise to take time to get some 'life experience' and expand your world view. The discernment journey continues for each of us as we go about our everyday life.

My smooth child-brain could not yet conceive of the wisdom in this refusal.

'So!' I huffed. 'This nun thinks that I, the world's most advanced sixteen-year-old, don't have enough "life experience" to make a lifelong commitment? Even though my school report card said I was mature for my age, which she'd *know* if she *asked*?'

I decided to play the long game. I'd go to university and study something – anything – just to tick that silly 'life experience' box. When I finished the degree, I'd be at least nineteen years old and, by then, I would know all there is to know about life. That'd be enough time to complete 'spirituality'. *And* God would probably talk to me another ten times *and* flicker my lights. Sister Monica would be so impressed I followed through. I'd show *her*. I'd show them all.

,

Reader, I did not show anybody anything.

I'm sure it's of great comfort to people of faith everywhere that I didn't become a nun. Instead, I found a boyfriend. I remembered how much I like owning stuff, sleeping in and being a glutton. And while I believe in many things I can't see, especially when my eyes are closed, an interventionist God is not one of them.

But I'll never forget what it felt like to be bathed in the rich musical soup of people using their bodies to express a communal hope. A place where every person contributed the exact same amount – one voice – to share in one outcome. I've been chasing that high ever since. Seeking out deeply felt, communal experiences has become my religion and choir is my favourite way to worship. Using my singing voice with others is my connection to something divine.

Choir is heaven on earth.

MISOPHONIA

I love silence so deeply that, for the unacquainted observer, I could understand if I come across as a bit psychotic. Listening to music to relax? *I would never.* Taxi driver wanting to chat? *Let me out, please. I'd rather walk to the next city.* The worst criminal sentence for me wouldn't be solitary confinement; it would be living with 500 other people, all clattering their canteen trays and making their loud prison banter.

My intense dislike of noisy environments may seem surprising when you consider that, for a living, I run what is essentially a noise club. At Pub Choir, I professionally encourage large groups of people to sing (yell) together. The reaction of each audience dictates what I'll do and say next, so I listen intensely to as much as I can throughout each show. To me, sound is information. But by the end of the show, as the crowd performs the harmonies I taught them, I've reached information overload. Sometimes, my ears feel so fatigued post-show that I'll slip away unnoticed while the rest of the crew chats excitedly in the greenroom, until a sense of quiet returns to me.

The world is a noisy place, so unfortunately, I'm not always able to hide inside a cupboard to avoid human interactions. Instead, I bring earplugs wherever I go. I have earplugs in my pocket, my wallet, my car and every bag I own. At home, I have multiple pairs positioned strategically in each room. If I ever don't have earplugs within arm's reach, know that I'm considering holding my breath until I pass out.

I believe that as a society, we've become obsessed with giving every human variance a name and a diagnosis. So, of course my aversion to sound has a medical title: misophonia. But knowing this name does nothing to help me. There's no medication or any ethical way to cure the world of noise. All I know is that I'm excruciatingly, unreasonably distracted by the sounds of other people being alive.

I once briefly saw a psychologist who claimed to specialise in helping people 'live with' misophonia. Which to my credit, I had already been doing for thirty consecutive years. But I was intrigued enough to book a session. I tried explaining to him that I feel this eternal, infuriating, toxic optimism that everybody around me will realise that *they* are making too much noise, and that out of a sense of duty to *me*, they will stop. But they never do. While I spoke, this psychologist cleared his throat every eight seconds, so I never went back. The nerve of him.

Maybe he was trying out some kind of clever, subtle exposure therapy, but for me, the entire world is exposure therapy. I can surround myself with people clearing their throats for free. So I opted out of his office, and opted in for earplugs.

Wearing earplugs is me admitting that I know other people have the right to make sounds because they're alive. I get it, you all need to breathe, to eat, to cough. I wish you *wouldn't* do any of these things near me because their sounds make me incandescent with rage, but even just writing this sentence reminds me that I'm in the wrong. So I wear my earplugs.

If you see me wearing my earplugs, please don't be offended. You can interpret them as a visible admission that I know I'm a madwoman, and I am trying to contain my own fury without resorting to violence.

For clarity, here is a non-exhaustive, ever-expanding list called: 'Reasons I Might Be Wearing Earplugs'. Subtitle: 'I Am Unwell.' Sub-subtitle: 'Sorry Everybody.' It's important to note that none of these rules apply to me because the sound of me being alive is delightful.

1. You are mouth-breathing and I can hear your breath catching on your throat. Please breathe through your nose.
2. You are nose-breathing but there is a whistle in your nose. Please blow your nose.
3. You are blowing your nose. Stop spreading germs. Please do not make me sick.

4. You are sick. You're coughing, sneezing, sniffing. Please see a doctor.
5. You are sighing continuously. Please see a therapist.
6. You are yawning. Please seek caffeine.
7. You are repetitively crinkling some kind of food packaging. Please give me some of your snacks, or quit your bragging and put them away.
8. You are making me aware of some dryness on your body: scratching your skin, picking your nails, licking your lips, itching your scalp, cracking your joints, clearing your throat. Please moisturise and hydrate.
9. You are slurping a liquid. Your mouth is a very capable hole. Please expand it.
10. You are chewing with your mouth open. Your mouth is a very capable hole. Please close it.
11. You are chewing with your mouth closed, but with such internal pressure that your cheeks and tongue recoil noisily each time you masticate. Please return to the cow pasture whence you came.
12. You are eating so quietly that I've become aware of the scraping and dinging sounds of your cutlery and crockery. Please mask your noise somehow with music or sparkling conversation (perhaps the only helpful piece of information in this whole rant).
13. You are mindlessly making percussive noises – clicking, tapping, jangling, jiggling, beat-boxing (this last one is a particularly heinous crime). Please save up all this rhythmic energy and join a performance troupe where

you and other like-minded fidgeters clang everyday objects like bin lids and spoons to wow your audiences. I will not be in attendance.

If you, or anyone you know feels personally victimised by this list (sorry to my partner Evyn), please accept my heartfelt apology.[1] Conceptually, I'm happy that you are all alive and making these noises, and promise to continue wearing my ear plugs to abate my own rage. It's definitely a 'me' problem.

---

[1] My apology does not extend to anybody who makes any of these noises inside a cinema.

ALTER EGO

In my first year of high school, during some sticky summer lunchbreak, all the students piled into the gymnasium to watch an aptly named 'heat' of the school talent contest. We sat in our hundreds on the hard basketball court floor, sweaty arsed and pimply, to watch five acts take the stage. Their confidence spanned from 'lacking' to 'misplaced', as did their talent.

First, a girl in a black leotard and glittery top hat gyrated some vague choreography to an emotional ballad. The next student scratched at a violin for a few minutes. Two sisters Irish-danced very well. Another duo took to the stage, with one friend singing shakily and the other occasionally strumming the guitar in a way that sounded more of flesh than note. Finally, a girl brought the house down by powerfully singing a Disney song to a karaoke track. She won the heat.

As an audience, we were enthralled with every act. We clapped and cheered if anybody survived their own performance. Even the untalented were given rousing applause for simply letting us gawk at their struggles (and indirectly helping us feel superior to them). But there was an electricity in the room if a performance even resembled 'good'. I greedily watched a small gang of students crowd around the winner, heaping her with praise. I wanted girls to crowd around *me* and say nice things.

I'd also never seen an audience respond to live music before. When I played the piano or the violin, it was for my teacher, the congregation at church or a music examiner. None of those scenarios involved a round of applause when I finished a song. To me, music had two sides: you could play music and hate it, or you could listen to music and enjoy it. But never both at the same time. I was surprised to see the kids at school show such a positive reaction to live music-making. I'd thought the only musicians who were celebrated for performing were the popstars I heard on the radio.

As a tween, I listened to the radio every single weeknight. From 6 to 10 pm, Kyle and Jackie O hosted my favourite show as they counted down the 'Hot 30' charting Australian songs, interspersed with a lot of inane, sexist chit-chat. As an adult, I can recognise how horny, mean and self-obsessed the presenters were, but when I was twelve, I was also horny, mean and self-obsessed. I hung on their every word. At least once a week, I tried to write down all thirty songs in order. Without money to buy CDs, I'd track my favourite songs and record bootleg copies of them on cassette tape. (Yes, I am that old.) I'd then replay my tapes over and over, while handwriting the lyrics onto brightly coloured sheets of paper to stick on my bedroom walls.

I loved hearing listeners call in to talk with the hosts and decided to try it for myself. One night, after an invitation was given to share opinions of a new song in a segment called 'Rate the Music', I dialled the station's number. Like all gambling origin stories, I had a win on my first try. A chirpy producer named Mummajugs (what a beautiful time in feminist history) answered the phone and asked for my name. I was placed on hold, then suddenly, I was a character on my favourite show.

'And now, we have Astrid on the line in Brisbane. Astrid, how would you rate the tune we just heard?'

'Oh my gosh thank you so much for having me I love your show so much I listen every night I'm so excited hi to all my friends listening I just loved the new song ten out of ten I just love everything you play WOOOOOO!'

It was a word salad. It was carnage. But those suckers sent me a free promotional CD as a reward for speaking on air.

So it was their fault, really, for everything that followed.

When an invitation was given for callers to rate the music the following night, I again dialled the station. This time, I couldn't get through. I punched the numbers in a second time. *Beep-beep-beep:* engaged. I called again, again, again . . . no luck! *Was I dialling too slowly? Could I type the numbers faster?* I decided to put the radio station on speed dial. I deleted whatever was in slot number 1 (probably something dumb like an emergency poison hotline) and programmed the radio station as the top spot on the family phone. Now, this button would do the work for me. As soon as I heard the first engaged *beep*, I could hang up and instantly redial. In the time it took one song to play, I could call the radio station forty times.

I didn't get through every night, but when I did, I squeaked a few words down the phone and would receive another free CD. Around my ninth or tenth time on air, Mummajugs recognised my name and address.

'Hold on . . . Didn't you win a prize yesterday?' she interrogated down the phone.

'Who . . . m-me . . .?' I stammered, caught out. 'Oh? I think . . . I think I might have won my first CD sometime last week,' I lied, mindful of the haul that I admired every night, spread out on my bed like goblin treasures.

Mummajugs sighed. 'You can't call again for a while, okay?'

'But . . . how long do I have to wait before I can call back?'

'Well,' she paused, 'it's not like there's a *rule* or anything. We just can't have the same listeners calling every night, so just . . . yeah, I dunno. Leave it for a while, okay, sweetheart?'

I stroked my chin and formed a plan.

The next night, I used my Crackhead Speed-dial Method™ until I got through to the station. This time, however, I used a different name. I was 'Conor', the name of one of my real friends from school. Conor went to air and won a CD. When asked for her address, I gave Mummajugs the details of Real Conor's house. The next day at school, I explained the situation to Real Conor. A few days later, when the CD arrived at her house, she brought it to school to give to me. Another treasure for my stash. As a reward for Real Conor's loyalty, I gave her nothing. It was the perfect system.

I tried not to hit up the same house too often. I mixed it up. A few days later, I'd be 'Shannice'. And then Real Shannice would bring my loot to school. Then I was 'Ngaire', 'Kelly' and so on through my classmates. One fateful day, I decided to be 'Keira'. This cover version of my very real, actual best friend called in to rate the music. After casting Keira's vote on air, an unplanned question to one of the hosts popped out of my mouth.

'Um, Jackie O, can I ask you . . .' I squeaked. 'In the ad break, there's this ad and it sounds like your voice. Is that *you* talking about pads and tampons?'

Jackie O laughed uncomfortably and said, 'Yes . . . Yeah, that's my voice, sometimes to keep the show on air we get asked to promote products and—'

I cut her off. 'Oh! It's fine to make some bucks on the side! I just wondered if it was you, is all. Get those tampon dollars, girlfriend!'

She laughed. She cackled. Both hosts laughed their commercial radio laughs where all their teeth were audible. Somebody probably played a *cha-ching* sound effect. This unexpected interaction was apparently radio gold.

When Fake Keira came off air, she wasn't only offered a free CD. Mummajugs said, 'Hey Keira, great job tonight! Can I call you in the future if we need somebody last minute to go to air?' Every one of my made-up personalities and I would have done anything for Mother Jugs.

So I handed over Keira's phone number. Which was my family's home phone number.

Thus began my nightly patrol of the family phone. I had to keep the line clear in case the radio station called. Did one of my brothers want to call some girl from school? *Go write her a letter, you unromantic tool.* Oh, Dad wants to call his mum in New Zealand? *Give that poor woman a break! Didn't you just call Grandma eighteen months ago?*

I tell you what, my phone militarisation strategy was necessary because the radio station did call. *A lot.* Keira was hot property. I intercepted the calls in time so as not to get found out by my family. I'd pick up the phone with a non-committal 'Hello' and I was always at the ready between the hours of 6–10 pm to respond as Keira.

Keira rated the music every other night. She introduced little segments. She said, 'Thank you for listening,' at the end of the show. Anything Mummajugs needed, Keira would provide.

But one day, a call came through to the house at 4 pm, *before* the show. Unprepared, I answered the family phone with my standard, 'Hello, this is Astrid speaking.'

'Hi sweetie, this is Mummajugs from the radio. Is Keira there?'

Oh no.

'Um, yes, I'll . . . I'll just go get Keira for you . . .'

Fuuuuuuck!

'Ah! Wait!' she said, throwing me a lifeline. 'Before you go, I actually need *two* people for some voiceovers tonight. Are you two sisters?'

No way, she's handed me the explanation!

'Yes! Haha. Yes, I *am* Keira's sister. That's me, alright. I'm Astrid, the sister of Keira!' I said in a super-convincing and normal way.

'Awesome! I need to pre-record some introductions for different show segments tonight. Would you like to do one together, make it feel like a fun party time?'

I tried to think quick. 'Oh my gosh, I would have *loved* to help, but I'm actually just heading out the door for netball practice, damn it! But I *will* grab my sister, whose name is Keira, okay?'

I held the phone at arm's length and stage whispered, 'Keiiiiiiraaaa! Phone for you!' I placed the phone down carefully, tiptoed a few steps away, then retraced those steps while stomping my feet like the elephant in the room Keira had become. But as I reached for the receiver, I realised, *We've got the same voice!*

I don't remember where I learned this bit of wisdom, but you can tell when somebody is smiling on the phone, even when you can't see their face. I smiled maniacally. 'HELLO! Keira here!' I said, as if in a hostage video.

For the next two years, I was trapped in an egotistical cycle of passing the phone from me to me. Keira was my 15% more enthusiastic sister, but Astrid was now also involved. They were never available to speak together at the same time. It was a delicate scheme, but the result was a doubling in scam productivity.

Over two years, I (we) swindled *hundreds* of promotional products stamped with 'Not for Sale'. I won an enormous denim jacket that fit nobody in my family. I was sent horrible but expensive sunglasses, signed posters and *So. Many. Free. CDs*. At the height of my powers, I helped two brothers win a free trip to Sydney to meet the popstar Sophie Ellis-Bextor.

Best of all (and take notes, children, because here is the moral of the story): I was never found out. I got away with *everything*. It was the perfect crime!

The relationship fizzled out mutually. Mummajugs called less and less, and Astrid/Keira stopped speed-dialling because we'd found a new obsession: the school talent contest.

After I saw that first school lunchtime heat, and the way the students responded to even the vaguest whiff of talent, I wanted that glory for myself. I marched up to the sign-up sheet and put down my name for the following week's heat. I didn't even have a talent in mind, I just knew I needed to do something.

That evening, I consulted my bedroom walls, covered in those brightly coloured sheets of handwritten lyrics. I carefully mulled over my options. I knew all the songs incredibly well, but I needed to find the right one for the occasion. Then I saw it: 'A Thousand Miles' by Vanessa Carlton. With one of the most iconic piano riffs in pop history, I felt shiny the moment I considered learning it. I ferreted around for my cassette tape recording, double-checked the first note of the song and then ran downstairs to our family piano to see if I could work out what to play.

In this moment, something shocking happened.

I touched the piano and realised I already knew how to play the whole song, even though I'd never tried before. I had listened to the track so many times while writing out the lyrics that I simply . . . remembered it? All of it! Sitting on our carpeted piano stool, I muddled my way through the whole song. Then I played it a second time, but with less hesitation. My fingers knew where to go and when to move. I knew all the words. I was singing and playing the piano at the same time and . . . What was happening?!?

It had never occurred to me until that moment that I could create my own versions of my favourite songs. All that music wasn't stuck in my cassette tapes or my ill-gotten CDs, but was malleable and alive. My favourite music was bubbling away in my brain, waiting for an outlet.

One week later, I performed in front of a crowd for the first time in my life. I was the youngest student in the whole school. I was almost invisible onstage behind the grand piano – something I'd never touched before. But as I played that iconic opening piano riff, I heard gasps of delight ripple around the room. Three minutes later, after singing the song through and tinkling the final notes, everybody in the gymnasium stood up and clapped, cheered and roared. *For Astrid.*

LESSON PLAN

At many high schools, the music department shares a classroom with the drama department. In every school I've taught at, these two weirdo subjects are on a rotating schedule to share the room up the back of the school that has three carpeted walls. The fourth wall has floor-to-ceiling mirrors. Everything smells of feet, thanks to the drama kids.

Whenever I had a music class scheduled in this toey space, I aimed to arrive a few minutes before my students so I could orient their desks and chairs to be facing away from the mirror wall. I knew my teaching abilities were less powerful than a self-conscious teenager's desire to stare critically at themselves in the mirror. To save them the grief and distraction, I would deliver my lessons to the students but also to my own reflection behind them. As a little treat to myself, I could pretend to look down a TV camera lens and break the fourth wall every time I made a sarcastic remark, like I was in an episode of *The Office*.

Anything to get through the day.

As I was rearranging all the furniture before an afternoon lesson, a student arrived alone and early. It was a school rule that kids were forbidden to have their phones with them during the school day. Yet here she was, blasting music through her headphones as she sauntered in and slumped down in one of the chairs. Rather than making her wait outside and put her contraband technology away, I thought peacefully, *This poor child. Maybe this is the only three minutes she's had to relax all day. She deserves a rest. Go on, little lamb. Listen to your music. Your secret is safe with me.* As the rest of the class filed into the room, my angelic early bird hit pause on the music she was listening to, tenderly rolled her headphones around her phone, replaced it in her pocket and loudly declared, 'I fucken hate music.'

I turned deadpan to Camera 1 (the mirror wall) then back to this little toad. *I fucking hate it more than you do*, I wanted to say. But when you're a teacher, you're supposed to be in charge and have a mature, calm reply for everything.

'If you hate music, why were you listening to music when you came into class today?' I said, my eyes quickly flicking to Camera 2 to double-check I looked as authoritative as I felt while delivering this comeback.

She was ready for me. 'Yeah, I like *listening* to music, but I hate *learning* about music.'

I had no comeback for this.

I know exactly what you mean, sweet girl.

,

I initially loved the experience of making music as a kid. Music ran thick through my veins. By age two, I was already playing the piano quite well by ear. I'd listen to my older brothers' piano lessons then toddle over to the piano once they'd finished, intuitively playing the songs they'd been struggling to master. I wasn't some prodigious talent, I just understood what to do. I was whipping through Suzuki piano books and sawing my way through violin repertoire before I could read words.

Money was extremely tight for my parents, and paying for five children's music lessons was no joke. So when my family moved from New Zealand's North Island way down south to a small town called Gore, my music lessons stopped. I don't remember caring too much about this, because we lived next door to a farm and had a magnificent garden. I spent my time climbing trees and chasing our pet lamb, rabbit and pig. Nature *is* music. I was getting my fill.

When I was eight, my dad got a job in Australia. My family left Gore to start a new life in a place called Brisbane. As an adult, my dad has since recalled to me that we were so poor at this time, he'd try to remember the features of any bridges he saw in this new city, should the family become homeless and need shelter.

So *how* did they afford my violin lessons? I wouldn't find out for twenty-three years.

Mum said to eight-year-old me that I was a very lucky girl, who would be having lessons with an expensive violin teacher every week. One of my older brothers, Phillip, had already started learning with this teacher and reported that she was magnificent.

Mum agreed. 'You *must* try your best and work very hard for her, okay?'

I couldn't believe my good fortune. Mum, who worked extraordinarily long hours, told me she would make time to drive me to and from my lessons every week, because they were so important. I promised to practise.

I lied.

These weekly solo sessions became my personal torture. I loathed my violin teacher and she loathed me. Let's call her Ms B.

Every week, I would hang my head in the back seat of the car, off to the gallows for my hour of scheduled crying. Mum would drop me at the front of Ms B's house. I would follow a stone pathway around to her back garden, where I would enter her teaching space through a glass sliding door. I'd set down my case on the cold, white tiles of her studio floor. I'd take out my violin as slowly as possible, pretending to tighten this and polish that. Sometimes a burst of optimism would kick in, and I'd ask long, smarmy, open-ended questions about music theory in the hope I could get her ranting and distracted. I needed to kill time.

'Ms B, in the music theory homework you so *kindly* set for me, I noticed I had mistakenly notated some consecutive 5ths in my harmony exercises. I went to play them at the piano – to learn from my mistakes – and I was surprised at the sonic beauty of the chords. Remind me, *why* can't we use consecutive 5ths at cadence points?'

Sometimes she'd take the bait, and we'd go on little conversation detours for five or ten minutes. Just once, I heroically managed to avoid playing the violin for an entire lesson. Bliss!

Usually, though, I was delaying the inevitable. The moment our dry conversation turned to dust, I'd have to prop my violin under my soft, sad chin. From the first note, I couldn't hide any longer: another week had gone by and I hadn't practised enough. That made, what, four years in a row now?

Unlike my bow, which dragged across my violin's bridge, Ms B's retribution flowed very smoothly.

'You are the laziest student I've ever had! How *dare* you waste my time with this rubbish. Even the dumbest of my kindergarten students could play this simple passage. How are you twelve and *this* much stupider than a five year old?'

She wasn't being rhetorical. She would genuinely wait for me to answer questions like this and I could never think of anything to say. 'Why are you stupid?' is a really hard question to answer, especially if you're stupid. And I'd never met these mythically gifted toddlers against whom I was always being pitted, so it felt impossible to compare and contrast our mental capabilities. Great chasms of silence would split open and she would let me fall in.

These days, if somebody heckles me onstage (thankfully rare), I'm better prepared. Some of my favourite go-to lines,

which work with almost every unruly idiot who tries it on at my show, include:
- I'm no doctor, but I think we've found the arsehole of the group.
- If you're looking for the show where everybody paid to hear you talk, it's just outside this room.
- We auditioned for the solos just before you got here, so sorry. You didn't get the part.
- I didn't realise it was bin day today! You're wanted outside on the curb!

Unfortunately, Little Astrid didn't have any one-liners prepared. It was so intimidating to stand there alone in Ms B's studio with no comebacks.

Every week, I would unsuccessfully pretend that I wasn't bothered by her emotional bullying. I'd try to focus on anything else but the prickle of emotions swelling up in my throat. My cheeks would burn, but I'd look past her eyes and focus on her hair. Ms B opted for a men's barber cut with the exception of a long rat tail at the back, which curled down and around her neck. I'd stare at her rodent hairstyle and see how long I could hold out.

Eventually, like the skin on her un-moisturised heels, I would crack. The discomfort of the situation would reach boiling point, and hot, shameful tears would trickle down my face. For this, I believe, was her goal: to break my spirit.

Playing the violin and crying are two entirely separate physical tasks. Once I was blubbing, she'd go through her exercises and I would comply. Forty-odd minutes later, I'd pack away my tear-splodged instrument and avoid it for another week.

Thank you for my lesson.

I'm sorry I'm so stupid.

C

    U

        Next

            Tuesday

Mum would be waiting for me in the car as I trudged out, swollen-eyed. I would say nothing.

I felt especially powerless because Ms B had been teaching Phillip before she took me on as a student. And she had taken to my brother like a rat with cheese. Phillip practised every week. He listened to violin music in his bedroom *for fun*. He was – and still is – enthusiastic, eager to listen and learn. As a student, he loved his violin lessons and Ms B loved him. As she should have. Their bond was so close that when Phillip went through his Catholic Confirmation process as a teenager, Ms B was invited to be his sponsor – to be a spiritual guardian in his life. She referred to him fondly as 'my almost godson'. In his final year of high school, Phillip stopped his lessons when he became busy as school captain. But there was Ms B at his graduation ceremony, seated next to me, radiating with pride.

My family respected her. Especially my mum. I didn't know why, I just understood it was extremely important to my mum that I do well in my violin lessons and not upset

Ms B. I felt guilty for wasting my parents' money. So I couldn't say anything.

Clearly, I was the problem.

To make matters worse, I kept getting high distinctions in every violin exam while Phillip – bless him – did not. It was almost like I *wasn't* the worst and most stupid person in the world. Maybe I was simply an infuriating student. I would sit for my exams and receive glowing praise from the examiners – for barely practising. And to be fair, I can imagine that it would be irritating to have your most disengaged student receive an A+ by following precisely none of your advice.

Ms B was the main character in my life for four years. In that time, I didn't take music as a subject at high school. I didn't join the choir. I played the violin in an ensemble at school, but I hated every second of it. I tried my best to separate myself from the thing I loved most. I was a pressure cooker packed with music but with no release valve. Ms B trampled the most natural, vibrant, fundamental part of me: she made me hate music-making. She made me hate me.

It wasn't until little Ms B was caught in action that things changed. Mum had dutifully waited out the front of her house every week to pick me up after my lessons. But one week, Mum couldn't make it. Dad was sent to collect me instead. Rather than wait in the car, he innocently decided to pop his head in to see what all this violin malarky was about.

And he walked in on a scene of destruction.

I was crying so hard I had crumpled to the floor and was hyperventilating, struggling to breathe. Ms B was standing over me, delivering some soliloquy about who knows what. Both of us turned at the sound of the glass door sliding open and saw my dad standing there, looking absolutely stunned.

She had been caught.

'What the *hell* is going on?' Dad demanded.

I don't remember what she said in reply. What could she say? The chaos was impossible to justify.

'We won't be having any more lessons here,' said my dad, as he hurriedly helped me to pack my things away.

My hands had gone numb from all the crying. Ms B watched silently as we scrambled to the exit. This was going to be hard to explain to Mum.

I know my mum was bitterly disappointed when I stopped learning the violin, for reasons that extended far beyond me; that crossed continents and generations. But from that day, I never had another violin lesson, and I haven't touched a violin since. My weekly torture was officially, suddenly, over.

I suppose because of the bond she'd formed with my family, and because I'd never voiced how she treated me, I was told to write Ms B a card to thank her for all my years of lessons. I was driven to her house one final time to deliver my note in person. I stayed in the car and watched as my physical body climbed out and walked to her front door. I saw my tiny hand reach out and knock very quietly. Thank *God* she wasn't home.

My trembling fingers slipped a card under her door.

Thank you for my lessons.
Sorry for being the worst.
Astrid

,

Teaching music is a unique challenge because music is fluidly woven into the fabric of everyone's life. Even people who've never had a single music lesson are musical experts in their own way. Every day, we add to our unique library of musical experiences just by visiting the shops, watching a movie or exercising with headphones. Music is everywhere. We use it to lock in core memories: 'Oh God, this song takes me back,' we cluck. Some mothers plan the songs they want to give birth to. There will be a playlist out there somewhere called 'Best Singalongs for Delivering Afterbirth', I just know it.

Listening to music makes us feel connected to each other, ourselves and our own lives. Listening to music makes us feel, full stop.

But learning to *create* music requires us to unpick all those feelings. To take what was a fluid experience and make it static. *Relax your pinkie finger. Stand up straight. Think about your breath. Count the beats.* For most of us, the moment we sit down behind a piano or hold a karaoke microphone, we realise the magnitude of distance between what we love listening to and what we can personally do. We feel inadequate to fall short of our musical heroes. And we feel betrayed that after all the hours we've spent listening attentively to their art, we still can't do what they can.

But I don't make music because I want to be a famous musician. I don't sing because I want to be the best singer – that's impossible. You can't 'win' at music, no matter how many tickets you sell. There is no finish line to artistic pursuit. Every exam mark, every eisteddfod, every award ceremony is an illusion. A subjective comparison of incomparable things. All art and music is an opinion. When you make music, you're not in competition with anybody.

I want to make music because music belongs to me. A musical instrument lives in my body for free and nobody in the world has ever had, or will ever have, the same one. I'm curious to discover the limits of what my instrument can do.

You too, without even trying, possess a unique musical instrument. When you sing, you are both the artist *and* the art. We can enjoy and admire many things as spectators in communion with others: sport, theatre, television, concerts. But when you sing, you experience a temporary conversion. Your ordinary human body becomes a living manifestation of music. No matter how weird or out of tune your voice is, there can never be another one just like it. Even a voice that's average at best deserves to be nurtured and explored.

Listening to music is worshipping at the altar of somebody else's talent. *Making* music is worshipping the unfathomable miracle of your own existence.

Anyway, that's the sort of thing I should have said to that kid in my class. But in that moment, it felt more important to be victorious in my conversation with a child.

So I stood before her and said to Camera 3 behind her: 'Tough luck, because complaining won't get you an A in the exam next week.'

And on I went with my lesson plan.

IT'S ALL RELATIVE

*C*an you remember the exact starting note of every song you've ever heard? Be it Beyoncé, Bob Dylan or Beethoven: if you sang what you recalled, would your notes be 100% spot on when compared with the original recording? Do you know the note your vacuum cleaner hums *before* you even turn it on? Congratulations, you have perfect pitch!

Also called 'absolute pitch', this is the equivalent to having a photographic memory for sound frequencies. Musicians with perfect pitch can listen to songs and transcribe the music with *complete certainty.* They can tune instruments to exacting standards using only their brains. They never sing out of tune and can point out whenever somebody else does. (This is a bit annoying, though.)

The benefits of having perfect pitch extend beyond music-making. You could slap watermelons at the supermarket and memorise what resonance suggests that the fruit is ripe. Oh, the dollars you'd save! You could pre-empt machine maintenance in your house, just by hearing a change in the electrical buzz of your dishwasher. I've read about a mechanic with perfect pitch, who could diagnose car troubles by remembering the note each model of car *should* be making. Something like 1 in 10,000 people has perfect pitch.

But not me.

I've always been able to figure out music in a way that sounds right, but might not actually be right. I'm the sort of performer who'd say, 'This next song goes a *little something like this*', and genuinely mean it. As a kid, I could instinctively figure out my favourite songs at the piano. When I wanted to perform 'A Thousand Miles' by Vanessa Carlton for my school talent contest, I had an intricate stencil of that song in my head: I could remember how far apart the notes were and how they all related to each other. I didn't automatically know what *specific* notes were involved, but I knew the overall 'vibe' very well. I listened to my cassette tape recording of the song then ran to my family's piano to match what I'd heard. I gave my rendition at school and it sounded correct (to 9999 in 10,000 people).

The thing is, our family piano was out of tune. According to that piano, the song was in the key of C. Twenty-two years later, I revisited 'A Thousand Miles' for a Pub Choir show in Sydney and was shocked at what I discovered. The version I'd performed at school had sounded correct to me. The ratio of notes I'd used was spot on, but in 2024 when

IT'S ALL RELATIVE

I played my (much better) piano against the original recording, it was carnage! A most disgusting clash of sounds where every single note I played was off by one place. It turns out that the song is in the key of C-sharp, which is an entirely different beast! Somebody with perfect pitch would never make this mistake.

The much shorter version of this is: I can figure out music in my brain very quickly, but not exactly. If you play me a song, I understand the relationship between the notes without needing to know what they are called. And as it turns out, this is perfect for my work with Pub Choir.

For every show, I arrange a different tune from scratch. I don't want audiences singing along with existing karaoke versions of songs; they could do that at home for free! 'Appreciating music' and 'making music' feel very different. I arrange new versions of well-known songs so my audience can *make music* together. To do this, I listen to the original song out loud while simultaneously imagining what else could sound good. It almost feels like remembering something I've never heard before: *How is it supposed to go again? What would sound right if I added it in*? I listen intensely to every song, almost like a meditation, waiting for new musical pathways to reveal themselves to me.

Some songs are *so* much harder than others to find a musical foothold. For example, I had to listen to 'Back for Good' by Take That for 392 minutes in a row before I heard the opportunity to add something new. Congratulations on a rock-solid song, Gary Barlow, but also *fuck youuuuuu*.

Generally, the time I need to make an arrangement will depend on how many extra layers I have to imagine. Two new vocal lines? Fantastic, I should have something ready by the end of the day. A string quartet as well? I'm going to need two extra days of song meditation. A full symphony orchestra on top of that? Clear my schedule for at *least* a week. It takes a lot of brain power to imagine thirty-six extra versions of an entire song.

Obviously, I'm bragging because I want you to be impressed but, more importantly, I want you to know this: I honed this ability by working at it for years. As in, it *is* possible to improve your musical abilities. I know, because I have.

Sure, I already had a head full of music before I got to university. I honestly thought everybody could harmonise with songs on the radio, or could play 'Clair de Lune' at the piano by ear. When I failed my audition for a Bachelor of Music course, I figured everybody else must be able to do the things I can do, and more. I didn't yet understand that the house of music has many rooms, and I was knocking at the wrong door.

I turned instead to the Switzerland of university degrees: a Bachelor of Arts. I wandered about aimlessly on subject selection day, looking for something to do with my life. Like everybody else, I signed up for a psychology course. I was still coming down from my Jesus years, so I also enrolled in a religion subject. Why not add biology – maybe I'd try to be a doctor so people would think I was useful? When looking to fill my last subject slot, I walked past the music department's stall. Manning the booth was a lecturer named Dr James Cuskelly, who was one of the adjudicators from my failed audition. He had 'priest on day off' energy – a clean, camp, friendly man whose crisp collared shirt was tucked into beige slacks worn with brown, woven-leather shoes. He waved in my direction. I turned around, wondering who was behind me. I turned back. *Was he waving at me?* I walked over.

'Hellooooo, I remember you!' he said, smiling so broadly that his nose crinkled and all his top teeth were revealed.

'Yeah, I'm Astrid,' I said, blushing at the thought that my audition was so awful it had stuck with him. 'I tried out for a place in the opera course. I was the one who . . . uh . . . sang something from *Phantom of the Opera* instead of actual opera.'

He laughed, but it didn't feel like it was at me. 'It was *great*, well done you! I hope you'll be taking my aural musicianship class this semester!'

Was this guy rubbing it in? 'I can't take your class, I didn't get into the music course,' I said flatly.

'Don't be a nong,' he said warmly. 'You can still take every single music subject you want to!'

'*Really?*' I asked.

'Sure you can! Come and join my class, I reckon you'll love it!'

I'd never heard of 'aural musicianship' before, but I enrolled anyway. It sounded like something to do.

In the first lecture, Dr Cuskelly announced that we would be training our musical ears. Something about 'audiation'. Edwin Gordon coined this term in 1975 to describe the sensation of using your mind's ear to imagine music that isn't actually playing out loud. 'Audiation is to music what thought is to language,' Gordon said. And I don't know how or why, but I'm top notch when it comes to audiation. I can't hear words in my head, but if I need to think about music, I can hear the whole friggin' lot.

But what can I *do* with this invisible skill? How can I get these thoughts out of my head and into the world in a way that is useful?

Enter: *solfège* (pronounced 'soll-fej' but where the 'j' is that fancy French noise, you know the one).

If you've watched the movie *The Sound of Music*, you might have briefly come across solfège when Julie Andrews sang the song 'Do-Re-Mi'. When I saw the movie as a kid, I had no idea what she was on about. But when I went to study aural musicianship at university, I learned how to harness this incredible tool.

At the risk of making your eyes glaze over, I'm going to launch into the *briefest* explanation of music theory, but I promise not to bang on too long.

Let me start with a small example: a major scale. I think most of us have some sense of what a scale is – a sequence of notes going up and/or down. When I learned my scales as a kid, they were presented to me using musical notation. For example:

IT'S ALL RELATIVE

This image shows the ascending scale of C major. I can look at those blobs and decode the information. I know which dots correspond to which piano keys, and I can play this scale with ease. But because I don't have perfect pitch, it's impossible for me to sing this scale with certainty using only my brain. I could check my notes against an instrument or some kind of note tuner, but I simply can't remember the sound frequency of the note C all by myself.

What solfège offers is an alternative way of thinking about this scale. Instead of using the note blobs, you can describe the same scale like this:

do re mi fa sol la ti do'

Instead of worrying about the *exact* sound frequency of each note (which is impossible for most of us), solfège helps us describe the *relationship* between the notes in the scale. Suddenly, it doesn't matter if it's a C major scale, an F major scale or any other letter, because knowing solfège allows us to understand the blueprint of a major scale. It is the stencil you can place anywhere.

Pause: I promise, this won't descend into a textbook. It's almost time to move on, hang in there!

Resume: Learning solfège felt as though I was an illiterate poet who had suddenly learned the alphabet. Now, I could write my poems down. I could think my musical thoughts and compose songs, and I could capture this information without having to find an instrument to verify the soundwaves. DO YOU KNOW HOW MUCH TIME THIS SAVES?!

The answer is: quite a lot.

Let's try it. Think of the song 'Mary Had a Little Lamb'. We all know how it goes. You could sing it if you were forced to. You might even be able to use audiation and imagine a version of it playing in your head. But if you had to *explain* the melody – say you wanted to write out instructions for your great-grandchildren to sing the song in their wasteland future, in which all instruments have been destroyed (don't overthink the reality of this scenario) – what words would you use?

'When you sing each syllable, the tune goes down, but then it comes back up. It's easy to sing, you don't have to move your voice very much, just a little bit at a time, and . . .' Very imprecise.

If you can read music notation, you might leave this instruction:

Ma-ry had a   lit-tle lamb

But this version isn't always true. You can start 'Mary Had a Little Lamb' from any note and it can still be right. And without perfect pitch, these notes are impossible to find using only your brain.

IT'S ALL RELATIVE

Solfège can accurately explain how 'Mary Had a Little Lamb' sounds without relying on the names of the notes:

"Ma-ry   had   a   lit-   tle   lamb"

mi   re   do   re   mi   mi   mi

| | | | | | ♩

It may not look like much, but the above provides every bit of information needed to bring the first line of the song to life. The top line shows the lyrics. The middle line shows the contour of the notes – how far apart they are using solfège. And the bottom line shows the rhythm – how long each note lasts. This recipe can suit any voice – it can start on any note and still be correct. None of it requires perfect pitch or a physical instrument to decipher. I look at this and, inside my brain, I can imagine exactly what the music is like.

That's the end of the lecture!

Hopefully, I haven't lost you with all this music jargon. What I'm actually trying to establish is the background information for how I came up with my PowerPoint presentations at Pub Choir. They're the centrepiece of my whole show. If you've attended Pub Choir in the last six years, you'd know that I am SO VERY PROUD of my PowerPoint slides.

I – me – Astrid Jorgensen – invented a way of demonstrating to my audience the relationship between every note they sing during the show. I teach a bastardised version of solfège to thousands of people at a time, and they don't feel a thing. You suckers!!! I worked out how to streamline and truncate everything I learned at university. For example, I'd transform the information in 'Mary Had a Little Lamb' into the following:

Ma-   **lit-tle laaaamb**

     ry   **a**

       had

This shows the lyrics, indicates where the notes go up and down (i.e. describing the notes' relationship to each other, like solfège), and gives some clue about the rhythm as you read from left to right. I call it a 'voxmap' because it visually maps out where and when your voice will move up and down. That's it. That's my contribution to humanity! It might not seem like much, but it IS. It really is!

I started voxmapping my arrangements about two years into Pub Choir, and I've been perfecting the idea ever since. I try to improve it at every single show. I colour-code different voice parts, and use all sorts of visual jokes for musical cues. *Nothing* makes me feel better onstage than a crowd cooing their approval for my instructional slides. Voxmaps are my way of visually presenting complex musical instructions to large, musically untrained audiences and Your Honour: I rest my case.

I am very excited to have made an intricate concept more accessible. I VALUE-ADDED SOMETHING TO MUSICAL

NOTATION. Unlike 'Pub Choir' the show, voxmaps can exist outside of me. I'm *actually* proud of myself. Bloody chuffed. Put it on my tombstone.

Fi-   **found some-thiiiiing**   **good**
    nal-   **she**   **to feel**   **a-**
       ly   **bout!**

Now, this point is crucial: I arrived at this idea because I practised *solfège* every day for years. I developed my audiation skills as much as I could. I enrolled in every one of Dr Cuskelly's ear-training subjects at university. I took all the homework he threw at the class, practised it on the bus, tapped my fingers at the dinner table and rehearsed in my head *constantly*. After three years of study, he'd helped me to literally name my musical thoughts. Mostly, Dr Cuskelly did what teachers are *supposed* to do – he helped me believe I was good enough to try.

I graduated my Bachelor of Arts believing I was a musician. It had nothing to do with my potential to be an opera singer, but everything to do with thinking musically. My best musical skill can't be seen or heard. It happens inside my brain.

As with everything in life, when it comes to audiation we all sit on a spectrum of natural ability. I'm certain most people think musical thoughts, at least to a small degree. Have you ever had a song stuck in your head? A jingle from a TV ad? A guitar riff from your favourite song?

That's audiation. The music is no longer playing out loud, but the earworm has burrowed into your mind. Your brain is hearing something, even if your ears are not.

You might think, *Okay, but so what? What does this mean for me?*

It means you can sing. Probably not very well, but I mean it more in a literal sense.

If you think about music, and you have the physical ability to speak, you can sing.

True, you might be spectacularly far from stage-ready. Perhaps you *do* sing very out of tune. I believe you! But if your only singing training has consisted of yelling songs in your car while stuck in traffic, what did you expect? A Grammy award? What steps have you taken to move beyond average? Being great at something is not a birthright. Somewhere along the way, we've become convinced that we can only ever be bystanders and consumers of the gifted, musical elite. I implore you to reconsider.

Yes, pitch is measurable. There's not a lot else about music that is so objective. If you want to sing the chorus of Adele's hit song 'Someone Like You', for instance, your vocal cords need to oscillate 440 times per second to create the soundwave pattern for the note A4. If your vocal cords move faster or slower than that, you'll sound increasingly out of tune depending on how far off your vibration rate is. Hitting the right note has a tiny window of opportunity, so try to be a bit kind to yourself if you miss (and don't ask somebody with perfect pitch for feedback).

IT'S ALL RELATIVE

The good news is, if you've *noticed* that you sing out of tune, this suggests to me that you have all the necessary components to sing *in* tune. Despite what many people seem to think, singing out of tune does not mean you're a permanent, fundamental failure as a person. It's not that deep, okay? You've just assembled your singing ingredients in the wrong order. You made a noise, you listened to your noise and you realised it wasn't the noise you had hoped for. But if you switched the order of these actions around, I think you'd have a much better chance of hitting the right note.

In other words, what about listening to the noise *before* you make it? What about using a little audiation?

Once you've sung a note, there are no take-backsies. The soundwave is already out there. You missed your mark and now it can never be unsung. That's the problem with singing and *then* listening. It's like attempting to play a game of darts blindfolded. You would simply never do that! Everybody knows you should look before you throw a pointy nail. You line up the tip of the dart with the board segment you want to hit, and you take aim with your muscles and your mind. *Then* you throw. I'd suggest doing the same for singing. Take aim for your desired note inside your brain, prepare your body to make this note, and *then* make a noise. That's how you sing a bullseye.

But just in case nobody has ever told you this: you're allowed to sing out of tune. It is not a crime. It's *okay* if you suck at singing, have no aspirations to improve and *still* enjoy doing it. If you're like me, our pitch can never be perfect. Let's just keep singing our notes – whatever they are – and planet earth will keep vibrating at its own frequency – whatever that is. Apparently, it's 7.83 hertz, which is an out-of-tune version of the note 'B' and, I mean . . . if the earth can't even hum in tune, you're all good.

STEADY HANDS

A conductor is the only musician who doesn't make noise. They control the noise of other musicians. A conductor silently shapes the passing of time by using their hands, face and body to communicate what they need from others, and when they need it. A conductor decides what the music means for everyone else. Conducting is perfect for creative, introverted control freaks.

I love conducting.

I had my first conducting lesson at a music summer school when I was seventeen. My teacher was Dr Anthony Young, an extremely precise, eloquent man with intelligent hands. He told the class to watch him and respond to his movements. Silently, he lifted his slender, pianist fingers in front of his body and shaped them as if he was holding a large imaginary orb. Everybody sat perfectly still, watching. Then, as if the imaginary orb had become too hot to hold,

Dr Young's palms leaped apart as he simultaneously drew in one quick, sharp breath.

Transfixed with his demonstration, I breathed in at the same time as him.

'Did you breathe in?' he asked.

My head snapped up. *Oh my God, was I that obvious?* Then I realised everybody else was nodding, too. What a relief! We had all subconsciously reacted in the same way.

'That was a cue. A silent movement that prepared you for action. I didn't need to tell you "In three seconds, I want you to breathe," I just cued your breath with my movements and you all breathed in.'

Holy shit.

Dr Young sang a note and instructed us to sing it back with an 'ah' sound. We obliged. His hands resumed their original position. As if rotating his imaginary orb, he stacked his hands vertically instead of horizontally. The top hand began floating up gently while the bottom hand remained still. Our 'ah' instinctively grew louder and more expansive. His top hand then did a small flourish, as if his thumb and pointer finger had pulled a small thread in the air. Our 'ah' immediately stopped.

This man is a magician!

The game continued. Dr Young cued us back in and, as one, we breathed and resumed our 'ah' note. He silently coaxed us to do all manner of complex musical things with this 'ah': making it louder or softer, singing it in short bursts, and even operatically. All by moving his hands.

STEADY HANDS

'Alright, now it's your turn,' he said, returning his magical arms to his sides. 'Stand up, and hold out your hands as if they're resting upon a large ball.'

Giggles erupted around the room as my classmates felt awkward in their own bodies. But for once in my life, I didn't feel uncomfortable.

Tell me what to do next, I thought. *Teach me your spells.*

A few days later, my classmates' giggling had turned to frustration as they mixed up their beat patterns and made jolty movements that were meant to look smooth. But I was confidently swirling my hands, cueing breaths and shaping the music – all without making a noise. Another student in the class slipped me a note that said: 'You are a captivating sculptress of sound.'

,

I can imagine I'm 'Pub Choir lady' to a lot of people. That's cool with me! Depending on who you ask, I might also be a child, sister, friend, boss or teacher. Maybe soon, I'll be an author in some people's minds (no pressure). If my identity to you is simply 'annoying', that's okay too (kinda rude, but I forgive you).

But I think of myself as a conductor.

I've never bothered claiming that as my identity out loud! I've not joined a conductors' guild (assuming there are such things, I couldn't be arsed to check). I don't study videos of Leonard Bernstein or wave my arms in front of mirrors or ... to be honest, I can't even think of another conducting stereotype. Because when it comes to conducting, I don't feel needy or like I have to prove myself. I don't care if anybody else sees me as a conductor, because I just I know I *am* one.

When I'm onstage at Pub Choir, my general goal is to teach (tease) the crowd until they know what to do without me. Everything is leading up to the moment where the audience becomes the performer. But that is also *my* moment of transformation: when I can stop talking about the music and start embodying it. How right it feels to shut my gob and resume my role as a captivating sculptress of sound.

AND I AM STRONG

'Are you sure you won't cry?' Marlene asked me as we walked into the church together.

Marlene, in her seventies, was impeccably dressed, with a long, black blouse and fitted black trousers. Her blonde-grey hair sat in a neat bob around her neck. She had a light covering of tasteful, subtle makeup – some foundation and blush – to smooth out her soft, papery skin.

I was eighteen and this was the first time I'd been a vocal soloist at a funeral. No, actually it was the second time – the first was at my own grandmother's funeral in Singapore. I'd sung a psalm called 'The Lord Is My Shepherd' and everybody had cried but me. At the time, I wondered if my family thought I was a monster for compartmentalising my emotions while I sang, but today it seemed like a positive attribute. Now, I was being paid $150 to sing for somebody else's grandma, whose family was farewelling her body for the final time. Marlene was to be my piano accompanist.

We had arrived at the church at the same time as the coffin. It was a rich, brown, shiny wooden box with an actual deceased person inside. I don't know anything about wood but, if I had to guess, I'd say it was made of mahogany because that sounds expensive. And the coffin really did look expensive. It had six heavy-looking brass handles and the lid was completely obscured by an enormous, elaborate bunch of flowers. Mostly lilies, I think? I don't know the name of anything.

'I'm sure I'll feel sad,' I whispered to Marlene as we sidled past the coffin. 'But I can't imagine crying for somebody else's grandma, who I never met. Wouldn't it be a bit weird for me to get so emotionally involved?' We put down our bags in the furthest corner of the church, near the piano. 'It just feels so . . . attention-seek-y to sob at a stranger's funeral.'

Marlene sat down behind the church piano and placed her fingers slightly askew on the keys. I looked at her hands – each finger was bent at a 45-degree angle away from her swollen, arthritic knuckles. She spoke to me over her shoulder as she warmed up her fingers by playing through one of the hymns. 'Well, the last singer had a lot of trouble stopping herself from crying during the final hymn and it really sounded a mess. Just be aware that it can happen. And when it does, it shifts the focus to us. But it's not about us, we're supposed to be here to help.'

Just as there are wedding singers, there are funeral singers – a fact that many people discover only at the worst time of their life. In Brisbane between 2008 and 2023, if your family was vaguely Catholic and your loved one died, I was probably there, singing 'Ave Maria' at their farewell. I've sung for at least 100 funerals, mostly with Marlene accompanying me on piano. We were such an odd, happy couple. We'd sit close together, listening to the eulogies, darting expressionless glances at each other whenever somebody said something controversial.

As an aside, Marlene didn't have a public funeral. When she died in 2023, even though we had talked for years about how we wanted our own services to go, I never got to say goodbye properly. (I miss you Marlene, I hope you don't mind living here as a little part in this story.)

,

I find funerals fascinating, grounding and spiritual – whether or not they include religious elements. They can be devastating, funny, awkward, cathartic and all manner of things, but they're never pointless. It's never a waste of time to bid somebody farewell. There's definitely an art to a eulogy, though. I've heard enough of them to confidently say that if you're given the unenviable, horrid task of eulogising a loved one, I encourage you not to read their resume and rental history.

So often, I've heard a person's life summed up by where they lived and what jobs they had. But how did you *feel* when they were around? Sure, you *could* list all the times your dad moved house . . . or you could retell that famous family story where he slid down the stair railing at the local pub trying to impress your mum on their first date, but it'd been so long since the wood was sanded that he got all those splinters in his bum and your mum had to pile him face down into a taxi and wait a fortnight for his arse to heal before they could go on their second date. And everybody will shake their heads and chuckle and say to each other, 'I remember that! He was always doing shit like that!'

Eulogies that give some sense of how a person lived and how they made everyone feel, really stick. I've heard incredible tales of men jumping fences to narrowly escape captivity. Of women who packed a suitcase and their two kids into a car and bravely started a new life. I've seen bereaved widows wail and beat their chest for all the love they had left to express. Angry children have spoken out about their unresolved trauma, and siblings have had everyone in stitches about that time their brother split his pants on live TV. Funerals are where I've learned the most about life and living.

Writing all this makes me sure that I'd happily still sing at funerals, if only I hadn't started receiving photo requests from members of the deceased's family and friends after the service. I *do not* judge anybody who has ever asked me for a grief selfie – I'm honoured you did. I'm more worried about myself (classic). What facial expression am I supposed to make while standing with my arm around a distraught Pub Choir fan, with a coffin as the photo backdrop? Smile with teeth or not? Sad face with a thumbs down? Will it end up posted on social media with the caption:

Said goodbye to Mum this morning ☹ but look who turned up to sing!!!

After the third or fourth time I grimaced awkwardly for one of these photos, I accepted that my funeral singing days were over. The only memorial service where I want to be a main character is my own.

One of the things I liked best about singing at funerals was that I believed nobody was looking at me. Unlike singing at a wedding, nobody films you at a funeral. There are no rehearsal dinners or behind-the-scenes photos. Nobody mails you fabric swatches of different colours a month before to make sure your ceremonial outfit brings the 'right vibe'. The vibes are low at a funeral. Not one person expects it to be the best day of their life. Ideally, nobody will notice you're there at all, because everybody is too busy grappling with their own mortality. Funerals are one of the last analogue, communal experiences we have. If you're texting or taking funny selfies during your grandma's eulogy, I'm sorry to tell you: you're behaving like a monster.

Because of funerals, I learned to sing with consistency and conquer my stage fright. Previously, I'd crumbled under the pressure of singing in public. Several times at school, I forgot the words to songs and cried the moment I came offstage. During university assessments, my voice would shake and I'd miss the notes. I felt like I could never sing the way I wanted to while I was being watched. But nobody was watching me at funerals. I found freedom in thinking about *how* I was singing. Up to that point, I realised I'd been singing *at* people, not *for* them. I'd treated lyrics like shapes and noises in my mouth, instead of words with meanings. At funerals, I started to view singing as a helpful service for the benefit of others.

And what helpful service did I think my singing was providing?

I was helping people to cry.

You wouldn't think anybody would need much encouragement to cry at a funeral. Not so! From my observations, the goal for many people seemed to be *avoiding* crying at all costs. There are cultural differences, of course (Italians seem to have public mourning down pat, for example). But mostly, I saw everyone working hard to hold back their tears. I've heard countless apologies from those who choked up during a eulogy. 'I'm sorry, I told myself I wouldn't cry,' they'd say, while speaking about losing the greatest love of their life. And if somebody managed to stay composed, you'd hear everybody pat them on the back as they returned to their seat and say, 'You were so brave keeping it all together.'

I'm not here to grief-shame; if holding back tears feels like the right thing to do, then please do that. Your grief is nobody's business but yours. But I would also gently say that, as a witness to many funerals, it does seem to be *exceedingly reasonable* if you want to shed a tear for the death of your beloved. I don't think it's embarrassing to love and miss somebody loudly. If anything, I think it's brave to cry first at a funeral, because it opens the floodgates for everybody else. Of course, grief isn't a performance, but you can feel some relief in the room if it happens: *Thank goodness, we can let out some of this heartache.*

For my first-ever booking as a paid funeral singer, I stared at Marlene's warped hands the whole time and I did not cry. After all, I'd never met the person who the service was for.

'You did really well,' Marlene assured me afterwards.

I beamed. As we left the church, I asked, 'Don't you think it's a bit sad that nobody cried for that woman today? Weren't they all the people who knew her best?'

'Next time we do a funeral together,' Marlene replied, 'try looking up and out at people's faces while you sing.'

At the following service, I braved a glance at the mourners. Nobody was looking back at me. Feeling empowered, I lifted my chin and sang out clearly. Then I saw it. The music Marlene and I were making seemed to offer some kind of emotional immunity shield to the people present. Not because we were amazing (we were, though), but because it's apparently an unspoken funeral rule that you *are* allowed to cry at a funeral during a song. When the melody swelled a little bit, and the lyrics and piano merged together just so, I saw stoic faces around the church creasing up with emotions.

This, I decided, would be part of my professional service. Singing for three minutes at a time so if anybody's grief was waiting for permission, my music would give it safe passage.

Sometimes (definitely not often enough), the task was made easier if the family chose songs that perfectly represented their deceased loved one. If Dad was a bit of a charmer who forged his own path in life against all the naysayers, and 'My Way' by Frank Sinatra was on the set list, there would be a tsunami of sobs. I'll never forget singing 'Smoke Gets in Your Eyes' at the funeral of a woman who loved smoking cigarettes and who died from lung cancer. She chose the song as a love letter to ciggies from beyond the grave. I remember thinking it was an iconic move to get everybody crying, laughing and frowning in equal measure.

Far more frequently, though, families dumped with the awful task of organising a funeral had no idea what songs their loved one would have wanted. (Please take this as your sign to tell the important people in your life what bangers you want played at your own service.) And this was where Marlene and I would come into the equation. Funeral companies would offer appropriately sombre live music to make the service feel a bit more personal. They'd send a list of tried-and-tested songs for the family to choose from.

Here are some of the most frequently requested hits:
- 'Ave Maria' (Bach/Gounod)
- 'The Lord Is My Shepherd' (If you need to choose between the Boniwell or Crimond version, always go the Boniwell.)
- 'Amazing Grace' (Traditional – this will become a sing-along which is always a good idea.)

- 'Time to Say Goodbye' (Andrea Bocelli and Sarah Brightman – I was equally bad at both parts. This is not something you can sing casually.)
- 'Make Me a Channel of Your Peace' (Prayer of St Francis)
- 'You Raise Me Up' (Josh Groban)

Whichever songs were chosen, I'd try to shape the words with intention and clarity, and *just* enough emotion that if anybody listening was holding back a sob, they could briefly let it out. It was always much harder getting a response from songs that had no connection to the person who died, but that didn't stop me from trying. Which is why at a certain funeral where nobody was crying, I did a crazy, stupid thing.

(I would start clenching your jaw now.)

It happened at a service for a much-loved husband and father. The church was packed to the brim. As always, Marlene was accompanying me at the piano. Everybody was trying to be brave and didn't want to be the first to break down in tears.

I'd sung my way through a couple of numbers, but every eye had remained dry. I was convinced that a communal cry was close by; it just needed the right conditions to surface. But I was running out of time to make it happen.

'Into your hands, O Lord, we commend our dear brother . . .'

The priest was already at the final prayer, which was my cue to approach the microphone. For the final song, as the coffin was to leave the church, the family had requested a rendition of 'You Raise Me Up' by Josh Groban – an absolute funeral classic. If you don't know the song, there's a section towards the end in the original recording where Josh Groban changes the melody in a dramatic way. For copyright reasons, I can't include the lyrics here, but they're along these lines: 'and **IIII** feel brave because of you'. It's the peak of passion in the song. If anything could dislodge a potential tear from somebody's eye, it's the way Josh sings that line.

The priest recited the final words of the service:

Eternal rest grant unto him, O Lord
And let perpetual light shine upon him
May he rest in peace.

'Amen,' came the dry congregational response.

Usually, I avoided risky notes and focused on singing as cleanly as possible for people to wipe away their private tears. But at this particular service, I felt it needed the big Josh Groban finish. Not one tear had been shed, and the coffin was exiting. Marlene and I had performed this song together loads of times before, always in the same way. But on the spur of the moment, I decided to give it some extra gas. As Marlene and I approached the all-important phrase, I squeezed my bum and went for it: 'and $\mathbf{I^{ii}_{ii}}$—'

My voice cracked mid-note.

It didn't just crack. It splintered with such force, I could have split the atom. It was a full Tarzan yell. If it were a scene in a movie, the editor would have smash-cut to a shot of the church roof where hundreds of birds were flying away in shock. Inside the church, my head jerked involuntarily in anguish as I tried to recover from this monumental yodel. But without drawing breath, a little joke slipped out. A comedy aside, whispered into the microphone. Automatically and without consulting my brain, my mouth said, as if in brackets, 'and I$^{ii}_{ii}{}^{ii}$ii feel brave (*not really*)'.

Like a scene from *The Exorcist*, Marlene's head swivelled 180 degrees in open-mouthed horror. Rather than the sound of sobbing, I heard gasps. I flicked my eyes quickly and saw that multiple people had turned their faces away from the departing coffin and were looking at me with hands cupped over their shocked mouths. I finished the lyric '. . . because of you', added in one final line of the song, then I *vanished*.

I exited the church at the speed of light. I have never moved so fast. I didn't stay to hear Marlene delicately finish the song, or wait for all the mourners to leave. Immediately, I was in my car, which had been sitting in the hot Queensland sun for the past two hours. I slammed the door shut and didn't turn the key. *Dogs die in hot cars.* I felt the excruciating heat inside the car pair with the hot shame I felt inwardly. I was distantly aware that I was moaning out loud and slapping the steering wheel with my open palms.

You idiot! Whyyyyyyyyyy?

ASTRID JORGENSEN

I'm not sure how long I sat there broiling, but I heard a quiet tapping on my passenger-side window. I turned and saw the WIDOW standing there. *Has she come to tell me my performance was like a second death for her family?* I leaned over and pushed the door ajar. Outside air gushed in. I gushed out, 'I'm so sorry for your loss and for, well—'

She cut me off by patting my hot, outstretched hand on the passenger seat. 'These things happen,' she said.

FUCK AROUND AND FIND OUT

Whenever I'm in social situations, somebody will inevitably ask me, 'So where did the *idea* of "Pub Choir" come from?'

I externally smile and mentally sigh. *I mean, really, where do any ideas come from?* I know I'm being asked to tell a dramatic, entertaining origin story and I feel anxious knowing that I simply don't have one.

It would be a relief if I could say I was struck by lightning. 'It was touch-and-go there for a while, but would you believe it, when I finally woke up from my coma, *I could SIIIIING!!!*' (These final words would be delivered as song.)

The real answer kinda sucks as a party anecdote. Nobody wants to be told that my cool job is the result of years of hard work. How disappointing is *that!* How do I explain succinctly to somebody's cousin the link between Pub Choir existing and me having sung at hundreds of funerals? It's too much to unload onto the curious, well-meaning stranger at the café that I can only perform so confidently because I scammed the local radio station for two years by pretending to be my own sister. So I usually just say, 'Oh! I used to be a school teacher, but I thought I'd rather be drunk!' and hope they chuckle and ask no follow-up questions.

In reality, I'm allergic to alcohol.

It's hard to pinpoint how Pub Choir came to be because it didn't arrive fully formed as an idea. It is *still* developing as a concept. Like all things in life, Pub Choir is the summation of so many tiny moments – many of which didn't feel important at the time. I needed to go through every embarrassment, to send every poorly worded text, and to fail, flinch and try again to end up with my dream job. My first Pub Choir event in 2017 bears almost no resemblance to today's show in 2025. My method of teaching, the venues, the crew, the songs, the technology – they've all changed and improved over time. The only constant ingredient has been me.

Yes, I coined and trademarked the term 'Pub Choir' to describe a musical experience with *me* as your teacher. Nobody had ever described an interactive event as 'Pub Choir' before, which is a verifiable fact that I welcome the eyes of my enemies to read while shedding their salty tears. But the show itself is a flexible idea that I continue to shape and stretch every day.

I know, *I know*, it seems an arrogant thing for me to say, but after eight years of experimentation, I've come to believe that Pub Choir is successful because of my unique skillset. The show is a demonstration of how I personally interact with music, and how I choose to share my thought process with others. People singing together is not new! Pubs are an old idea, and choirs even older still. But *my* iteration, where I improvise a comedy music lesson for 90 minutes for thousands of untrained strangers and teach them my original vocal arrangements from scratch, using a musical notation of my invention? Well. I've worked my whole life thinking up how to do that.

The phrase that comes to mind to describe my general outlook and motivation in life is 'Fuck Around and Find Out'. I know people use this phrase as a warning to precede violence, but I've reclaimed it as my own personal mantra to constantly try new things and eat little treats.

As far as I'm concerned, if you want to learn something, or to figure out if something is right for you, you need to try it (Fuck Around) and reflect afterwards (Find Out). Of course, this attitude should exclude doing crimes and unnecessarily being a dickhead to others.

Prior to Pub Choir starting in 2017, I Fucked Around and said 'yes' to everything and everyone, at least once. This led to exciting things, like saying 'yes' to a secret gig where I had to agree before finding out the repertoire, venue or date – and which turned out to be a gig conducting for the Rolling Stones (like, the actual band). And sometimes, 'yes' led me to hop into the back of a stranger's car with my brother Hugh (I was eight and he was eleven) in the middle of a thunderstorm.

Some nondescript Asian lady pulled over at the traffic lights and asked, 'Do you two need a lift somewhere?'

Hugh and I quickly conferred, and *swore* we'd seen her hanging out with our Singaporean mum. 'Yes, please!' we replied as we scrambled, sopping wet, into her back seat. 'Thanks for the lift, great to see you again . . . aunty,' we said, trying not to let on that we couldn't remember her name. Turns out, we'd never met this woman before. Luckily, she wasn't a child snatcher and drove us safely home.

Saying 'yes' has landed me a lot of jobs. The day I was legally old enough, I decided to Fuck Around and apply for a job at McDonald's so I'd have money to buy clothes that weren't hand-me-downs from my uncool brothers. There, I Found Out that all the grease in the air from the fryers gave me acne. So I worked in a bakery. There, I Found Out about getting fat. I was briefly a boarding house supervisor, where I had to wake up children to get them to school on time, and Found Out I'm not interested in parenting. Being a movie attendant taught me not to sit in the back row of a cinema without getting checked for an STI afterwards. Being a theatre usher taught me that I find opera incredibly boring. And so the list goes on.

Here are all the other jobs I can recall gracing with my presence:
- Classroom teacher
- Relief teacher
- Wedding singer
- Funeral singer

- Background singer in bars
- Voiceover artist for ad jingles
- Medical receptionist
- Dental receptionist
- School administration assistant
- High-school workshop facilitator
- Food-tester
- Medical drug trial participant
- Barista
- Cleaner
- Composer
- Conductor
- Original singer-songwriter
- Theatre script consultant
- Private music tutor
- Radio producer
- Associate on the board of a think tank
- Motivational speaker (ha!)
- Sales rep for a global bedding chain where I had the lowest sales average of any employee nationally. (I averaged $3, and not a single thing in the store cost $3.)

It's quite the list. Clearly, I've not always been a very loyal employee. The second I realised a job wasn't right for me, I'd make my escape. On to the next thing to see if I could find something that felt more 'right' for me. A typically self-important millennial attitude.

Also, I was determined to keep trying new jobs until I found one that wasn't shameful to discuss at a dinner party.

'What do I do? Well, I'm a singer-songwriter.'

'Awwwwww,' they'd respond as their heads rotated 45 degrees. 'That's cute, good on you for trying. Have I seen you on TV?'

'No, I . . . I play space-themed, jazz fusion songs and I only have one fan called Matthew, who is sometimes the only person who buys a ticket. So I generally spend more money on parking at the gig than I earn by playing the gig.'

I can see why they felt bad for me.

The most socially acceptable job I had before Pub Choir was working as a high school classroom teacher. For the first time in my life, I could tell somebody what I did for money without getting a sympathetic head cocked to one side.

Unfortunately, teaching was simply too hard.

You try and keep thirty teenagers seated, respectful and on task while droning on about the development of chromaticism in the Romantic period. You must hold your class's attention without resorting to teasing or swearing even once. And you can forget about toilet breaks or sitting down to eat lunch, because you'll be on playground duty, contractually spying and eavesdropping on children during their only hour of reprieve from you.

In the evening, parents will send you angry emails about your inability to reverse the behaviours they imparted to their own children. You also have 270 reports to write before

1950: June when she was 31 years old, Singapore.

1992: Astrid in homemade knits, New Zealand.

1992: Astrid behind the piano.

1993: Astrid playing dress-ups as a nun.

1993: Five siblings in hand-me-down clothes (*L–R*: Hugh, Astrid, Timothy, Malcolm, Phillip).

1994: A Jorgensen self-timer family photo (*L–R*: Hugh, Malcolm, Stephen, Phillip, Elvira, Timothy, Astrid).

1994: Astrid's first day of school (a year too soon) (*L–R*: Timothy, Malcolm, Phillip, Hugh, Astrid).

1997: Dylan and Astrid: pupils of correspondence school via the radio in Gore, New Zealand.

1997: The Jorgensen family celebrates Elvira's graduation from law school in Invercargill. (*L–R*: Timothy, Stephen, Elvira, Hugh, Astrid, Phillip, Malcolm).

1999: Astrid having an outdoors violin lesson in Brisbane, Australia.

2017: Astrid takes a selfie with the audience at Pub Choir's first show in Brisbane.

2018: Astrid's outstretched arm conducting Pub Choir's viral performance of 'Zombie' (The Cranberries) in Brisbane. *Photo: Jacob Morrison*

2020: Australian of the Year Awards (Queensland ceremony) Astrid with Jackie Trad.

2020: Education is freedom. Stephen and Elvira Jorgensen sit in front of their tertiary qualifications and those of their children, Brisbane.

2021: Astrid in her hi-vis and hard hat, pre-show at the drive-in cinema in Yatala.

tomorrow and you must never, under any circumstance, tell the truth in any of these.

In the morning, the first child you see will mutter under their breath, 'Here's this cunt again' as you walk towards them (true story).

The mental toughness of anybody who endures the teaching profession is incalculable. Every day in the classroom felt like I'd been booked as an entertainer for the world's worst solo gig that lasted from 8 am to 4 pm. The set list sucked, the audience hated me and nobody was listening. Teaching felt like yelling poetry into a jet engine: futile, but something to pass the time, I guess?

Thankfully in 2016, my partner Evyn received a yearlong hospital placement in Townsville, Queensland. With great relief, I took a year off classroom teaching and followed him north. I knew nothing about Townsville, and nobody who lived there. To me, it presented a clear opportunity: I had exactly one year to Fuck Around and Find Out what I wanted to do with my life.

I remember lolling about upside down on the couch in our temporary apartment, trying to think outside of the box. *Do I have any skills that are transferable to, like, the real world?* I compiled a mental list.

Astrid's transferable skills

1. **I'm good at multitasking.** Playing the piano while singing or conducting an ensemble of musicians requires

you to think of many things simultaneously. Outside of music, this means I can read a book and watch a TV show at the same time. Is that a job?
2. **I think really quickly.** I remember getting pulled out of class in high school for an aptitude test, and being told that I'm in the 99.9th percentile – three standard deviations above the average – for my speed of thought and processing power. This means I'm a weapon at the card game Snap. Is there some kind of job where you have to, I dunno, react really fast?
3. **I love to sit down.** Who wants to stand up all the time? What am I, on a diet? Big thoughts happen when you sit. Think of the years I've spent sitting and practising the piano or violin. The countless hours I've sat slumped in a choir chair, listening to the sopranos go over their part for the ninetieth time. My endless ability to sit quietly has been honed through decades of half-arsed (on my arse) effort. Does anybody need somebody to, um, sit down and think about stuff?

It was Evyn who suggested it. 'Why don't you look up becoming an air traffic controller?'

I flipped myself the right way up on that couch and got immediately lightheaded. 'What makes you say that?!' I panted.

'Well, I mean, I don't know *heaps* about it but I'm pretty sure the job is thinking quickly and multi-tasking while sitting down,' he guessed. 'Isn't it kind of like professionally playing a maths computer game except the goal of the game is, you know . . . keeping people alive?'

I scrolled some online forums. Air traffic controllers were describing themselves as multi-taskers. Quick thinkers. Who sat! One man portrayed himself as the sort of person who could sit at a noisy dinner party and retain the information from simultaneous conversations either side of him. I tell you, my family had been training me for that scenario my whole life!

I immediately applied online.

This began a months-long process of interviews and aptitude testing.

First, I passed the preliminary compatibility screenings. Then, I studied to sit a complicated two-hour exam that tested my mental maths ability, general scientific knowledge, and pattern recognition. Throughout this test, weird distractions kept happening with increasing frequency. For example, while solving a series of mental arithmetic against a countdown timer, a bunch of coloured shapes appeared on the screen for five seconds with no explanation. Three minutes later, while calculating 18% of $27, a question box popped up to ask: 'How many green squares were there?'

It was challenging, yet trivial, which is how I'd like to imagine people describing me as a person. I couldn't believe these little brain teasers were the entry barrier to a very cool, real job. I passed all the aptitude tests followed by the personality tests (verifiably not a psycho, thank you very much). By May, after an hour-long phone interview with

Airservices Australia, I was offered an in-person appointment. The final step. I booked in my timeslot for a fortnight. It was all becoming real. I was going to leave music behind and start a new life as an air traffic controller. I was looking forward to being a less pitiable guest at all future dinner parties.

That very same week, I received a fascinating email from a stranger called Katherine. She was the head of music at a local high school in Townsville. Now one of my dearest friends, Katherine had an ambitious idea: a whole school choir. The school in question, St Patrick's College, wanted to find a conductor to lead a compulsory choral lesson, which would be forced upon every single student. I was intrigued. We arranged to meet for coffee.

'What's the choir *for*, exactly?' I asked, sipping my iced latte and feeling a trickle of sweat between my cheeks both top and bottom. (Townsville is oppressively hot.)

'Nothing,' Katherine grinned at me. 'It's a choir about nothing!'

'Okay, Seinfeld,' I joked. 'But there must be a reason for it?'

She laughed. 'The school just wants a positive, creative experience for the kids. Some togetherness. An hour of teenage girls not bitching at each other and making music together instead?'

Some tiny cog of recognition turned in my brain. *Music to feel connected. How novel!*

'I mean, I'm interested. I just . . . can't understand how you even found me?' I said incredulously. I'd barely left the apartment in five months, convinced that I needed to prepare for my life as an air traffic controller.

'I know your ex-boss in Brisbane,' Katherine divulged. 'I asked Danny if he knew of anybody who moved up north recently, and he was so excited to give me your name. He said you're fantastic and also that you'd be spookily perfect for this project.'

Another little cog clicked into place in my brain. *I am right for something.*

Sitting across from this endearing, Disney-eyed woman and her well-placed flattery, I tried to think of reasons not to do it. 'Um . . . how many hours of work would it be?'

Katherine sighed. 'That's the bad news. Whole school choir would only happen one hour a fortnight. Plus an hour of paid preparation time. But I *promise* you could build more work out of it. There's no singing teacher at the school but some kids want to learn. Only a tiny handful of girls are in the non-compulsory choir but we've got a huge number of kids from Papua New Guinea and the Torres Strait. And let me tell you, for the right person, they are ready to sing.'

Every time I'm at a decision crossroads, if one of the options has somebody enthusiastically waving me over, I'll go that way. It's not very brave, but validation is one hell of a drug. Down one path was air traffic control, where I had the chance for a completely fresh start and could forget about all my previous exploits. Down the other path was dogshit pay, but somebody saying, 'I believe in you. You are right for this. Would you like to build something together?'

'Can I just try it and see how I go?' I asked.

A week later, I was walking out in front of all the students and staff in the hideous Townsville heat to the sound of 500 pairs of eyes rolling back in their skulls. Honestly, can you imagine yourself at fourteen, sitting through an hour of school assembly, only to be told that it was now mandatory choir time? That you'd have to sing in front of your peers, and nobody was allowed to leave? You would've sprained your face for the cringe.

To prepare for my first whole school choir session, I'd written out a lesson plan of what I was going to do and say. I didn't look at it once. I don't remember what I said, and I don't remember what I did. In fact, I never remember the specifics of what happens when I conduct a choir. I am a woman possessed. When I'm in front of a choir, I'm in a flow state. I feel like I can see the musical destination clearly, I just have to convince everybody to come along for the ride.

By the end of the first whole school choir rehearsal, the whole school had become a choir. Loads of kids signed up for the opt-in choir. And quite a few wanted private singing lessons from me. I was building something, just like Katherine had promised. And I wasn't just building work, but self-belief. Every fortnight, one hour at a time, my confidence grew. All those strange jobs and the underwhelming, weird experiences I'd collected had led me to this place of intuitively knowing what to do and say to get 500 people singing together.

I cancelled my air traffic control meeting. For the first time in my life, I said 'no' to a job before I even tried it. I had properly Fucked Around with the idea, but I never Found Out. Because there I was at whole school choir, using my transferable skills:

I was multitasking. *Tick!*

I was thinking quickly. *Tick!*

Unfortunately, I needed to stand up to take the rehearsal and have been on my feet ever since, but two out of three isn't so bad.

JAW-DROPPING

'Sing the same phrase again, but this time, drop your jaw down a little bit. Give the notes more space in your mouth, and a little less tension in your jaw.'

I'm sitting in a tiny office above a high school gymnasium, half-heartedly delivering a singing lesson to a Year 10 student from behind my janky, electric piano. The thumping and clacking of the cheap, plasticky keys recoiling as I press them is louder than the sound of her voice. She's preparing for a vocal exam next week, and we've been practising the same songs every week for three months.

Teaching somebody to sing can be a tricky task, because the instrument is invisible. Honestly, that element of singing is pretty annoying. Unlike playing a piano, or *any* other instrument, you can't see or touch your singing voice. You can't look down at some keys or press some buttons to make specific notes; singing comes from within you and you're the only one who can expel it from your body. This becomes more challenging to master if you feel self-conscious and nervous, which is how every single singing student feels. Most of my lessons involved me trying to convince somebody to relax, and that I wasn't going to laugh at them (not in front of them, anyway).

If you manage to get over the awkwardness of singing in front of somebody else, you can start concentrating on how your singing feels. *That's* when you start improving. Singing is a physical activity; any noise you make can be physically explained and even counteracted. Everybody has good and bad days – the trick is remembering how you felt when your singing sounded good, then re-creating that physical state on demand. To me, learning to sing means reliably configuring your body to make consistent sounds.

Having such a perfect understanding of the sensations you feel is difficult for anybody at the best of times, let alone when you're a pubescent kid who feels like they're being held hostage by their alien, ever-changing body. It's hard to remember how you placed your tongue in your singing lesson last week if, in the time since, you've grown a weird new patch of hair and you're pretty sure your right leg is now longer than your left.

So here I am, in this cupboard of a room, listening to my student nervously rehearse her same songs, which she manages to sing differently every time because she has so little control over what is happening in her unfamiliar body. I wonder how I can repeat my instruction without making her feel judged. 'How did your jaw feel as you went for that high note?' I try.

She tells me her jaw felt tense and she also doesn't think she put enough air behind the note. 'Okay, sing it again and *only* think about your jaw. Just concentrate on one feeling at a time,' I say, with a smile on my face that has nothing to do with her (sorry, kid). I do try to be very present in singing lessons because they're a vulnerable experience for everybody involved, but on this occasion, I'm distracted. I've had a late night. Such a late night that I didn't sleep at all and now yesterday has merged into today.

My student readies herself to sing the same phrase again. I try to refocus my eyes on the tiny notes in front of me. I need to convert the black musical blobs on the page into electrical brain signals that tell my fingers which piano keys to press. But I'm too hot and tired, and I keep making mistakes.

'Sorry!' I breezily tell my student. 'I'm just finding your performance so beautiful I can't play the right notes today!' *Will she really fall for this?* 'Let me find a backing track so I can free my hands from the piano and listen to you more deeply.' I'm essentially looking for a three-minute break. I'm so tired I might as well be hungover. (I'm not, to be clear.) I find the backing track on my computer. 'Okay! Sing for me your best version of this song, exactly how you're planning to perform it for your exam next week.'

'It makes me feel so nervous that somebody will be sitting there, staring at me and judging my singing!' she says, limping her weird-feeling legs around the room.

'Well . . . that's sort of the whole point of an exam: having somebody judge you. But I tell you what . . . I'll pretend to be your examiner now! I'll listen all the way through and give you feedback at the end, yeah?'

She nods and sighs deeply, steeling and stilling herself for this dress rehearsal. I click 'play' on the backing track and slump back in my chair, hoping I appear to be respectfully looking at my hands in my lap. In reality, I'm just relieved I can hunch my shoulders for three minutes. It's a lot of effort pretending to have good posture in front of your singing students. This brave girl clears her throat, preparing to launch her body into the song. *I should really tell her some other time not to clear her throat just before she sings.* I close my eyes to listen and immediately my brain starts wandering outside of the room.

Last night was Pub Choir's first show. I haven't slept a wink. My student is warbling something in the distance. *Oh my God, did my life change last night?* My mind is drifting.

A few months prior to this slack and sleepy singing lesson, I was sitting on the floor of my apartment with a university friend, Meg. It was January 2017. I'd just returned from a year in Townsville where I'd had the transformative experience of leading a compulsory whole school choir of 500 singers. It was the most exhilarating job: figuring out how to conduct such an enormous group. But now I was back in Brisbane where nobody wanted a whole school choir.

Meg and I reminisced about how we and all our classmates had sung together in every lecture for three years at uni. But the moment we graduated from our respective degrees, all that glorious music-making disappeared. Now, Meg was working in the unmusical corporate world, and I was dragging my feet back into the classroom. Is twenty-seven too early to be so depressed about your career?

While I was still making a lot of music, none of it was for me. Alongside teaching high school music, I was working as a private vocal tutor and running six community choirs each week. I would have loved to ditch the school stuff and work exclusively with choirs, but you can't pay a mortgage *and* buy food *and* petrol from six weekly rehearsals. I had to teach classes during the day and singing lessons in my lunch breaks if I wanted to support my choir-conducting habit. Morning until night, I zigzagged across the city, taking rehearsals, lessons, classes and more rehearsals. Once a fortnight, I'd even drive to the city of Toowoomba to conduct my favourite choir, Choirbolical (reigning best group name).

'Choir is what I want to do with my life,' I told Evyn, and anybody who would listen to me, to explain why the skin under my eyes had gone such a weird grey colour. Deep down, I knew I was running myself ragged, and that my chaotic approach wasn't going to bring me the choir life I wanted. The only full-time choral jobs are for people offering something extraordinary, which I was not. I was just offering *a lot*. And none of it felt authentic to me. I was pouring all my musical energy into schoolchildren or semi-retirees – both groups who deserve music and who I loved working with, but who didn't reflect twenty-seven-year-old, foul-mouthed, adventurous me.

I wanted to make music with my peers. I desperately wanted to stop pretending that I was serious, authoritative and self-assured to teenagers. I am none of those things. It was all a lie. I needed a way to make music that felt true to me. I'd experienced it briefly in Townsville directing the whole school choir. Where was that opportunity for grown-ups?

Where was the choral invitation for people like *me* – adults who make wisecracks during rehearsals under their breath? The sort of people who really love music, but not enough to wear diamante treble-clef earrings. Which choir can you join if you feel too embarrassed and uncoordinated to learn choralography (choral choreography for the uninitiated)? What if songs by cheesy, 1990s boy bands make you feel happier than Mozart ever could? What if you *really* want to get better at singing, but you're too embarrassed to audition for a choir or to attend a singing lesson? Or what if you just can't be arsed going to a rehearsal every week because you're busy, and you never stick to anything. Where can you go if you just want to feel briefly connected to other people, without worrying about committing to something and ultimately letting everybody down?

Pub Choir was the answer to all these questions.

'Imagine singing one song in a pub with cool casual people and then just . . . pissing off afterwards?! No performance or rehearsals, just a one-night stand with a song?' I said to Meg, as we ate dry falafel on a picnic rug in my apartment with no furniture. 'I'd definitely go to a choir rehearsal like that and maybe some of our friends would too?'

We started listing the names of mutual friends we thought we could bully into joining a social choir. We could easily think of at least ten people! *Ten people is enough for a choir, right?* Our shared excitement grew. Meg knew a venue that might agree to hosting a pub singalong event. I knew a song I wanted to arrange, and how I'd teach it. Was I too busy? *Fuck it!* I thought. *Why not take on a seventh choir and chuck it in the pub? I'll call it Pub Choir!*

Meg contacted a pub called The Bearded Lady where she'd been hosting a poetry slam for a few years. She convinced the owners to let us use their back room for two hours for a rowdy choir event – phenomenal! I had the phone number of a female guitarist, Waveney, who I'd worked with in 2014. We hadn't stayed in touch, but I remembered her being very funny, with a great musical ear. So I texted her for the first time ever:

Hey Waveney, it's Astrid! How are you?
I was wondering . . . Would you like
to do a crazy pub choir project with me?

She wrote straight back with an enthusiastic 'yes'. Waveney's willingness to go on this musical adventure with me (an almost-stranger) felt perfect. The pieces fell into place quickly, and nothing gets me focused like external pressure from others. Meg had the pub at the ready. Waveney was keen for the gig. So I locked in my arrangement then wrote this post on Facebook, nine days before the first show:

HEY EVERYONE. I'M SO SO EXCITED TO ANNOUNCE PUB CHOIR! I'M YELLING THIS ENTIRE POST.

This is a choir for ANYBODY. No audition, no concert, no sheet music, no pressure, NO WORRIES!!!! Every month I'm going to teach one well-known song at the pub (Bearded Lady) and at the end of that night we'll perform the whole song in 3-part harmony. We'll film it, post it, then NEVER DO IT AGAIN. A song one-night stand.

Waveney Yasso is going to accompany me – she is a guitar and percussion wizard, and Megan Bartholomew (of Ruckus poetry slam glory) is MCing.

Bring your mum, bring your brother, bring ya gran, just probs don't bring your baby because it's in a pub. We gon' get druuunk to relax!!!!

Hope to see you there!

Side note: my event descriptions aren't booze-focused these days, but please understand I was trying to convince my fellow broke, mildly depressed musician and teacher friends that this weeknight event would be fun. Getting drunk was the best card I had to play, okay?

Just over a week later, I was at The Bearded Lady. I'd come straight from school and was wearing my teaching outfit: drab grey clothes but with a funky brooch to impress the kids (never worked). I didn't know who'd be coming to the show. I'd chosen to teach the song 'Slice of Heaven' by Dave Dobbyn, which is very 'pubby' and wasn't a song I'd heard any choir perform before. And that's the message I wanted to give to whoever turned up: *this is choir reimagined!* I'd arranged my three-part harmony version in my head and had sent Meg some lyrics to print off and hand out. I'd also asked if she knew anybody who could film the show, because I thought we should capture whatever happened on video. Apparently, some twenty-year-old videography student called Paris was going to come and film the show for a couple of free beers. I hoped she was nice.

Entry was $5 cash. Some friends started arriving and milling about the bar. I tried clocking everybody who came through the door: *There are two music teachers I went to uni with. Oh, there's a woman I used to give singing lessons to! Hey, he's a singer-songwriter, that's cool of him to come! Wait . . . who are they?* I had assumed the room would be filled with people I knew. But strangers on the street saw the chalkboard sign out the front that simply said 'Pub Choir $5' and started sticking their heads in for a rubberneck. We ran out of lyric sheets very quickly. *One between two, that'll be okay!*

ASTRID JORGENSEN

I chatted to Waveney and Meg about nothing, trying to pretend I was relaxed before the show, in case any of these strangers looked over at me and decided to leave because I was clearly too flustered. *Oh my God, seventy people have turned up for this chaotic choral experiment.* Feeling sick with nerves, I turned the grey colour of my teaching clothes.

Showtime rolled around. Meg went onstage and seemed confident. She was saying things to make the audience more excited. I think? I couldn't comprehend anything because I was so anxious. She must have said my name and introduced me, because she was pointing at me and people were clapping and looking my way. My legs felt like they were made of concrete. Was my right leg suddenly longer than my left? I grinned, then limped onto stage and picked up the microphone.

Wed 12th April – Brisbane – 11:05pm
[my actual diary entry]

I'm finally taking a moment to record what was undoubtedly one of the most exciting experiences of my life so far! I had to work all day today and was so distracted I couldn't concentrate! Last night I led the first ever session of Pub Choir! An idea I had in January finally came to fruition. I was so, so, SO nervous beforehand. I think mostly because I knew how much potential this idea has. 70 actual people showed up. A lot of them I knew, but some I'd never seen in my life!

JAW-DROPPING

I taught 'Slice of Heaven' by Dave Dobbyn to seventy drunk strangers in 1 hour! In 3-part harmony! The really exciting thing was that, despite being painfully nervous beforehand (did someone say nervous poos), the moment I stepped onto stage, I felt <u>totally</u> at ease! I can't even remember what I said, I just . . . knew what to do to get everybody singing? I think I was born to do this! The joy in the room was palpable. People were ecstatic to be singing. To me, it was an insane success. The way everybody cheered the moment the song ended . . . I'll never forget it. So much joy mixed with surprise and accomplishment. What a beautiful noise!

I've barely slept in 48 hours. I feel like a drug addict coming down from an incredible high! I'm sure this is the beginning of my life as I was supposed to be living it – I was made for this shit! Everything I've ever done came together on that stage. I am so proud of myself and so very optimistic about where this idea will take me. ARGH!!! PUB CHOIR!

I'm embarrassed at how earnestly I wrote this diary entry to myself (and how many exclamation points I used). But in my defence, I didn't think anybody else would ever read it. And when it comes to my intuition about the show's potential, I was right. My life really was going to change. I had no idea that a few years later, I'd deliver a live, televised singing lesson to 200,000 people on *Australia's Biggest Singalong!*

Or that I'd teach 102,947 people around the world to sing 'Bohemian Rhapsody'. I certainly didn't expect to perform in front of a sitting prime minister on Australia's most legendary music TV show, *Spicks and Specks*. All I knew was that I'd had a great idea and my life had changed for good.

The morning after my life changed, I dragged myself to school and put on another grey ensemble with a quirky feature brooch that nobody noticed.

And now, I'm sitting in my vocal teaching studio, smiling at the thought of how special I feel. But . . . somewhere in the corner of my mind, I realise the backing track is no longer playing. I am sitting silently with my eyes closed, hunched behind the piano, asleep in the middle of a singing lesson. *How long have I been out!?!* I open my eyes and look at my student, who is standing there awkwardly, not knowing how to wake me up. It might've been five seconds, it might've been five minutes. *I don't think anybody should be paying me to be a singing teacher.* (And they won't for much longer.)

'Sorry for, uh, being a little quiet at the end of your performance,' I tell her. 'I was just . . .' I bow my head, as if consumed with emotion. I look up into her eyes and with Pub Choir in my mind I say, 'I was just taking a moment to process how beautiful all that singing was.' We smile at each other for our own reasons.

MANSPLAINING

Q: Where does a man get his water?
A: (A well, *actually.*)

Near the bottom of New Zealand, there is a town with a few thousand people called Gore. In the centre of Gore, there is an enormous statue of an upright trout fish, and . . . not a lot else. In 1997, my family moved to Gore after my dad got a job as the deputy principal of the local high school. My mum also got her first non-nursing job here, as a freshly qualified solicitor of family law.

I attended the local primary school, but it was apparent I was a bit ahead of the rest of my class (#gifted), so I was also enrolled in correspondence school. Like a Babushka doll, there was another school within my school, but this one was via the radio. A few days a week, I would leave my class and head for the library where I'd pick up a headset and radio receiver and attend school of the air.

These radio lessons were delivered to thousands of children in regional areas all over New Zealand. We'd tune in weekly to hear our mystery teacher's voice. The crowning glory of correspondence school was that, once a term, I would be sent a personalised package with all the work I had to complete. A nerdy gift parcel addressed to Miss Astrid Jorgensen. Oh, how my hands trembled with excitement as I tore open ten weeks of homework. All for me!!!

Previously, everything I had was a hand-me-down from my older brothers. I'm talking undies, too. What a handsome young lad I was. It's no wonder that at age four I looked around the family dinner table one night and asked my parents, 'Um . . . when will I be turning into a boy?' Whether it was my brothers' clothes, their manky old toys or even just their preceding reputations, I was perpetually in their shadow. 'Another Jorgensen child!' everybody would proclaim. 'Are you as clever as your brothers?'

Well, not yet, I'd think to myself. *They got a head start.*

Everything my brothers did, I did too, but later. By the time the fifth child gets an A for their piano exam, it isn't so much of an impressive achievement, but more the meeting of a bare minimum expectation.

To attend correspondence school and receive homework gifts in the mail made me feel incredibly important. I lorded it over everyone. I'm sure this made me very popular in my physical class. *Fellow children, I must retire now to the library to take some correspondence. Best wishes, kind regards.*

I interpreted my peers as being impressed, when I'm sure it was a sigh of relief I heard as I left for the library.

One memory from this time that remains clear in my mind was a radio lesson that had me visualising myself in a hot air balloon. 'What do you think you would see if you were so high above the ground?' the voice of my teacher asked us, her chosen airwaves flock. 'Imagine the view from a hot air balloon and then write it down for me for homework.'

So I wrote the following poem:

When I am high up in the sky
The world below is passing by.
The houses look like little toys
For all the girls and all the boys.

It's no Mary Oliver, but I mean . . . come on. I was seven! I felt proud of it and read it to my siblings. They couldn't believe it. As in, they didn't believe I wrote it.

My brothers turned on me. 'YOU didn't write this, you copied it from somewhere!' accused Malcolm.

'Whose poem is this and where did you hear it?' Timothy interrogated.

'I didn't copy it! I wrote it!' I banshee screeched. 'I wrote it all by myself! It's not even that good!'

They stared me down and as one, they jeered, 'There is NO WAY you wrote this poem.'

I don't know if they were simply teasing me, getting me riled up like brothers tend to do. I've always been easily outraged and maybe this was just a funny game to them: to piss me off and pass the time. If so, it was very effective. But I remember the feeling of a small, hot rage inside me that fortunately/unfortunately (depending on how you look at it) has never diminished.

I was telling the truth. I had done something clever, and they said they didn't believe me. Was it was because:

1. I'd done something better than they could do?
2. They didn't care either way, but were simply trying to expose me as weak-minded.

And this crossroad is where mediocre men have been irritating clever women since time immemorial.

To be fair, my brothers have, in fact, become very kind, clever, respectful adults. I can't say the same for all the men I come across in the music industry. I'm not trying to implicate anyone or take anybody down, this is simply a statement of fact: very often, the cool dudes I come across through my work with Pub Choir don't understand that I'm the person in charge. It's not even that these blokes refuse to believe I'm the boss, but it simply hasn't entered the realm of possibility in their minds. And I refer specifically to men, because men are by far the predominant employed species in music venues, and if you've played a gig, you'd agree. In eight years of performing around the world on hundreds of stages, I have only encountered two (2) venues that were majority run by women. (Hello, Thalia

Hall in Chicago, and The Crocodile in Seattle, you are the promised lands.)

Look, of course, worse things are happening in the world than sound guys rolling their eyes at each other knowingly when I ask them to stop changing the settings on my gear without being asked to. But they definitely do that sometimes. And it annoys the living shit out of me. Or they'll soundcheck my microphone so it perfectly suits their voices, even though I insist that the mic should be tweaked to suit my voice (because I'm the person performing the show). I've heard myself described as a 'meddler' when referencing how I wanted to attend *my own soundcheck*, which made me clench my hysterical, girly fists. I catch lighting rig operators snickering backstage when they see the PowerPoint slides I use to teach my (sold out!) audiences what to sing. They assume that, because my show looks simple, it is stupid. I then assume that *they* are both of those things.

I don't say anything out loud, because it's not the cleverest move to piss off the people who control how well the audience will see and hear you. (Don't worry, the ones I'm talking about won't read this, or maybe any book.) So I stand there, with my clotty uterus and inferior mind, and nod as a man with inexplicably wet hands describes how I should hold a microphone. I let these hilarious lads laugh at my gear and ask me questions like 'Are you musical yourself?' while *I* set up the chairs for the symphony orchestra that is about to perform the score I wrote. Venue guys love to give me advice on how to improve my show without knowing a single thing about it. And they *constantly* ask me when 'the choir' is coming to soundcheck, despite me explaining for the third time that it is the audience who *will become* the choir.

If they talk to me at all, that is. More likely, the staff will address the men in my crew as 'Sir' and ignore my existence altogether. Even worse, they'll touch the small of my back whenever they walk past me on their way to ask the boss (a man, who isn't the boss) a question. To be fair, it's probably better they don't talk to me, because 'being polite to venue dickheads' has really gone down my list of priorities over the years.

Anyway. During Pub Choir's first year, I was too overwhelmed to notice these small episodes of misogyny and was definitely not experienced enough to counteract them. I had 500 people lining up in the rain to see my show and I was distracted, overwhelmed and working my arse off. So it took me some time to realise that venues, and occasionally even colleagues, weren't always speaking respectfully to me.

About eight months in, I realised I needed help. Offstage, I was doing everything. I'd arrange the songs, build the website, promote the shows on social media, book the venues, sign the ticketing contracts, track down the song publishers, edit the audio, pay the crew ... and *then* I'd perform the show. But so much worse than all of that, my personal phone number was attached to the website. And the only people who prefer to call instead of sending a succinct text or email are the people you don't want to get a call from. Every time somebody wanted to book Pub Choir for their event, or discuss payments, or complain about the song choice, they rang me *directly*. If an entitled audience member wanted to complain about the aesthetic of the carpet in a venue's foyer, it didn't feel right that they had a direct line to the lead performer. I needed a barrier.

And out of my fiery, feminine anger, the weapon of Kirsten Aitken was forged.

I've since realised that this name felt so real because it *is* the real name of an existing TV newsreader on the ABC. (Thankfully, her family name is spelled differently so I hope she was never implicated in my mischief.) I must have absorbed her in the back of my mind because I often have the news playing while I work at home. But in my moment of need, I believed that I'd had a brilliantly original idea to invent an employee called Kirsten Aitken, who was to become Pub Choir's assistant, who was also . . . me.

This wasn't my first alter ego. After years of pretending to be my own sister to swindle CDs from the local radio station, I was well versed in playing a character. This time, I stepped it up. I bought Kirsten a SIM card and a burner phone. I registered her with a company email address. I put Kirsten's contact details on Pub Choir's website and put Astrid's phone on silent. We both stared at her phone and waited.

Kirsten was a bright, chirpy woman with a thick New Zealand accent (my childhood also prepared me for this), who could say everything Astrid felt too scared to say. If somebody rang up to complain, they no longer had free rein to chew my ear off, because Kirsten would jump in with statements like: 'Let me take your feedback to the team so they can talk it through.' But the team wouldn't talk it through because the team had been on the call the whole time. Kirsten also negotiated much better deals. When Astrid wanted to say, 'I would rather eat glass than split $50 between three people for two days of work', Kirsten would simply say, 'Thank you so much for getting in touch about your event. Unfortunately, your budget is not a good match for the team's world-class skill levels.' Side note: a fake assistant is a great way to give yourself affirmations.

Kirsten was a friendly, bitchy, business assassin, and I loved her. Sadly, I had to let her go because there were two problems she couldn't solve.

First, she wasn't there to help me in person at a show. She was a great defender of Astrid via email and phone, but when some pushy man spoke down to me at a venue, only I was there to cop it in real life. I needed somebody to help me in the physical realm.

Second, a journalist cottoned on. Kirsten was on her burner phone with her cheery Kiwi accent to arrange a media interview for Astrid, who was too important to be planning her own schedule: 'How does Tuesday work, I can see that Astrid has a 30-minute window available at 3 pm?' She didn't mention that Astrid had every 30-minute window available that day.

But this journalist kept pausing thoughtfully. 'Remind me again, what's your name?' she asked Kirsten, no less than three times in the phone call. She was sure she was speaking

MANSPLAINING

with Astrid (which she was) and kept repeating: 'It's so funny . . . so strange . . . you sound just like Astrid.'

In a panic, I repeated the lie I had used the last time my alter ego was caught out on the phone: 'We're sisters so that's why we sound so alike!'

Unfortunately, in almost every media interview I'd ever done, I'd mentioned that I only had brothers. This journalist seemed to know that fact. She went quiet and waited for Kirsten to admit that she was me, and that I was Astrid, and that we were both putting on a silly voice. I admitted *nothing*. It was too embarrassing to admit! I will never admit it. (I'm admitting it now.) The interview never went ahead. The jig was up.

Women, stick with me here. To solve both problems I hired a man. Not because I thought a man would be a superior negotiator or anything. No! I wanted to outsource the experience of receiving 'mansplaining' in the workplace . . . to a man! I believe in this instance it's just called 'explaining' where all the men interrupt each other and offer unsolicited feedback and say 'Well, *actually*' to each other, and everybody else just gets on with their work in peace.

I found this gentle, giggly, clever man called John Patterson via an online ad, asking for somebody to work ten hours a week to answer my emails and media enquiries. And also to be a misogyny sponge (but I didn't include that in the job description). John – who is a famous rock guitarist who toured the world with his band The Grates before co-owning and managing a café and its staff – applied for this ten-hour-a-week admin job. I found his application confusing enough to be intriguing, and arranged for an interview. I hadn't understood the term 'overqualified' until that moment, but ultimately thought to myself, *Why wouldn't I want somebody who knew way more than what I asked for?*

Thankfully, John said he wanted the job. So now we've been working together going on six years and I truly think he was the second wind that stopped me from giving up on Pub Choir out of sheer exhaustion. I'd also note that his workload has extended beyond ten hours a week (cute understatement).

On his first day, I sat down with John and spoke at him using approximately a million words a minute:

'So the thing is, haha, um I need you to perform your own handover from your predecessor, whose name is Kirsten.'

'Oh! I didn't realise—'

I immediately cut him off and continued my induction ramble. 'Kirsten was my previous assistant who was, like, also a figment of my imagination. I made her up so she could negotiate for me on behalf of myself and she had a New Zealand accent but you don't have to be from New Zealand unless you are.'

'Right, so she—'

'So, yeah, now that you're my *real* assistant I need you to log into Kirsten's email, and hand over all her clients to John, which is you – haha, you knew that bit already – and then there's also this burner phone that Kirsten has been using and . . .' On and on I babbled.

MANSPLAINING

It was a smooth transition of power from Kirsten to John. They were both very good sports throughout ('both' being John at that point).

Apart from me, John remains the only other full-time employee at Pub Choir. Our motto is 'DIY or die', which I'm fairly sure is something John said supportively to me early on, probably when I was explaining the whole 'burner phone' situation. Now, I'm in charge of everything outwards-facing: what happens onstage, choosing repertoire, musical arrangements, creating the PowerPoints, social media (yuck), media appearances, writing all public communications and the whole performance thing. John is in charge of everything inward-facing: venue hire, event management, contractor scheduling, website maintenance, tour planning, merchandise, publishing negotiations, advertising, accounting and all manner of other things I don't understand.

In short: I think of stuff to do and John makes it happen.

We both believe we have the better job.

It would be remiss of me not to mention that Paris Owen and Jacob Sosnowski (my brilliant videographers) and Evyn Arnfield (my brilliant boyfriend) are the only other people who have been riding Pub Choir's rollercoaster since the very first show – predating John's involvement. But don't worry, I know how my eyes glaze over when I see a list of names in a book, so I won't do any more of that now.

Plenty of talented people have been involved with Pub Choir over the years – I'm excited to introduce them in stories or thank them at the end of this book. But it's time for me to move along and spill some more secrets, because this is starting to read like a bad Oscars speech. The band is playing me off.

I suppose what I really want you to know, after all that, is that at every Pub Choir experience – the 7000-person shows at Riverstage; the overseas tours; the festival appearances; the orchestral arrangements; the special guests; the social media; the videos; the photos – they were *all* achieved in-house by a team smaller than most book clubs. There isn't a faceless cast of thousands behind the scenes. There is no Pub Choir machine, churning out impersonal content and trying to increase profit margins and smash KPIs or ... whatever somebody who knows about corporate finance might say.

No, the show is made by a handful of kind, slightly overstressed people, who are reading every comment, taking everything way too personally, and trying as hard as they can. All while selling more tickets domestically than most other Australian live music acts. In fact, I think Pub Choir actually *outsells* everybody else, but I don't know how to fact-check this and I'm too busy to look right now. And we do it all while slumped on the couch at home, texting each other things like:

> **Me:** *Do you think people would be weirded out if I hired a whip-cracker for the show?*

> **John:** *Only one way to find out. P.S. I'm putting the Melb show on sale tomorrow, can you please write a mailout?*

MANSPLAINING

Me: Ugh. Can you remind me in an hour, I have to finish this string quartet arrangement.

John: Sure. Also Paris asked if Pub Choir could fund her to take a lighting course so that she can snap back at lighting guys at future shows when they talk down to her

Me: YES. IT'S A YES FROM ME. Whatever it costs I will pay for that! DIY or die!!!

THE EVENT HORIZON

Whenever you feel overwhelmed by the relentless passing of time that speeds you towards your inevitable death, I suggest you book a performance. Not as an attendee, but as the entertainer. Pub Choir is a good middle-ground option because you're transformed from an audience member into a performer by the end of the show . . . but anything will do. Read some original poetry to your friends at a dinner party. Put on a ukulele recital at your family's Christmas lunch. Make your colleagues/enemies watch you perform interpretive dance. (This will be especially effective.) Whatever it is, in the moments before you start your performance, something incredible will happen to the space–time continuum: time will drag on. And on, and on, *and on*. Booking a gig is the secret to feeling like you have too much time.

The last 30 minutes before you begin your performance will magically last for seven hours. You now have time to check all your unread emails, send replies to those Christmas cards you received in 2019, and call back your car insurer about extending your policy. Two minutes before showtime, you'll be able to wander around aimlessly backstage for three business days. And when the clock finally claims there's one minute to go, you'll become trapped on the edge of a black hole where time stretches to infinity. Aptly named the 'event horizon', I can only assume a performer named this scientific phenomenon while pondering their own existence pre-show.

Standing behind the stage curtain and hearing excited audiences chatting on the other side, who all paid real money to be bossed around by *me*, is an intense, eternal feeling. Every single time, fear sweeps through me as I realise I have no script, no lesson plan and no clue what I'm doing. I stand backstage, asking myself, *Why did you think you could do this?!?* Then the paranoia kicks in. *What if I've forgotten how to speak, walk and hear sounds?* I imagine myself attempting to run onstage, then falling over and knocking out all my teeth. Or maybe this will be the night where my most frequent, recurring nightmare becomes reality: I'll walk onto the stage only to realise that nobody has come to the show, meaning I have to run back and forth as fast as I can, pretending to be 1500 different people so that Paris can film the video.

There's no way to find out *what* horrors are about to unfold until I start the show. And I can't start the show until that bloody second hand reaches twelve again, during which time I could gestate an entire human being for nine months. *Where did all this time come from!?*

I look at my watch and wait for the exact moment the clock strikes showtime. This is not an exaggeration – I stand still and stare at my watch. As the second hand hits 8 pm, 0 minutes, 0 seconds, I give the thumbs up to John, which is my visual code for: *If we don't start this show immediately, I will scratch out my own eyes, then yours.* Whatever start time the audience was given is the time I want to start the show. If the lights to my show don't dim exactly on time, know that something has happened and I am *stressed*.

Once at a show in Melbourne, somebody kicked out my laptop charger by accident during the soundcheck, which I only realised at 7.59 pm when my laptop died and the stage went black. The show was due to start at 8 pm, so the 5000-person audience cheered as if things were kicking off a minute early. But the lights didn't come back on for a full five minutes more while my laptop rebooted. Those 5000 cheers turned into sounds of confusion and impatience, which made me grind my teeth with a severity and tension that will only be released after the event of my death.

Yeah, it was only a five-minute delay, but from inside the event horizon, I felt like I'd been crouching in front of my computer's loading screen since the big bang.

When I'm running late for anything, I feel physically unwell. Really, there is only a one-second window to be truly on time for anything. Before that second is early, and after that second is late. We must be prepared for that briefest sliver of existence called 'being on time'. If you're not early, you're already late. The only exception to this rule is when you're trapped in the event horizon before your performance starts. You're neither early nor late because time has ceased to exist.

As with all sci-fi plot lines, there is a price to pay for the protagonist who experiences all this pre-show time-stretching. When you *finally* manage to step onstage after waiting for twenty-five years, time will move so fast that your two-hour show will be over before you've even finished saying 'Hello!' to the audience. Suddenly, you're offstage again, sweaty and confused and ... *It's all over? What happened out there?!*

I suppose that's why I put myself through all the turmoil and self-doubt. Imagine my relief to discover that the moment the show starts, I get a little break from myself and all my thoughts. Time flies by – I stop worrying about that varicose vein on my left shin and if everybody I've ever met is mad at me – and instead I spend two hours deeply listening to others, looking for ways to be helpful.

Of course, once I step offstage, my brain comes back online and my squirming begins.

'Did I . . . tell that New York audience to "build a wall"?'

Paris nodded apologetically. 'Yeahhh, Astrid, I'm not gonna lie. That's the loudest boo I've ever heard at your show.'

I could've sworn it was a normal turn of phrase and I was *not* using it as a political statement. But yes, I did tell 1500 New Yorkers to 'build a wall' (of notes) in 2019.

'Do you think they heard me say the wrong city when I said, "Great job, Brisbane"?' I asked my crew after a show in Sydney.

Madison, who had to translate the audience's booing into sign language, patted me sympathetically on the shoulder. 'Darling, even the Deaf heard you say it.'

'I'd like to start this show with a brief round of intergenerational trauma,' I confidently announced in Brisbane, before doubling over in shock at what had come out of my mouth. *Trivia.* I'd meant to say, 'Intergenerational *trivia*.' No, I won't be starting the show with a few quickfire questions about your abandonment issues.

I once introduced a politician onstage into the microphone as, 'Oh . . . *shit*,' upon realising I'd completely forgotten who they were.

I've made unfunny remarks about a virus sweeping the stage – I mean, I *was* talking about my computer, but the Covid timing of that joke was very off.

I've even mistakenly revealed to an audience I was pregnant – only I wasn't pregnant, I was reading aloud a funny sign somebody in the crowd was holding up. The sign said, 'Astrid, I'm pregnant!' and was in reference to an internet joke at the time. As I was exiting the stage at the end of the show, I spotted the sign and read it to the audience. They clapped and cheered with an earnestness that didn't match the style of the joke. I walked offstage, confused, until I realised: my audience believed that I'd chosen to announce my forthcoming child by speaking like a cave-woman then immediately leaving the stage. 'Astrid!' (with a finger pointed at myself) 'I'm pregnant! Bye-bye!'

The improvised nature of Pub Choir means I'm always saying something regrettable onstage – it can't be helped. The show requires me to respond in real time to whatever is happening, so I just have to live with whatever cringeworthy thing I've said to 1500 people in the spur of the moment. If a gig doesn't go perfectly, I'm stuck in a post-show time warp, remembering every stupid thing I said. And unfortunately, there is no such thing as a perfect show.

Well . . . that's not strictly true. There's no such thing as a *second* perfect show. Because I've already had one, and I don't want to be greedy.

My perfect show happened on 8 February 2018. When it was over, I celebrated. Time rolled on at its usual tempo. On that one occasion, I didn't feel silly about what I did or said onstage. I felt as free and happy post-show as I did onstage. It was the show of myth and legend.

It happened in Brisbane at a pub then called The Elephant & Wheelbarrow. It was a cloudy summer night and the outdoor beer garden was filled to capacity – 500 people were crammed into the concrete courtyard laced with fairy lights. Keith, the venue manager, was kind enough to construct a small, temporary stage at one end of the space, which elevated me and my accompanist Waveney about 50 centimetres above the ground. As we're both very short people, this extra height meant we were basically performing face-to-face with 500 regular-sized people.

THE EVENT HORIZON

At this point in Pub Choir's trajectory, I hadn't figured out my octave-displacer microphone. The lyrics weren't voxmapped (colour-coded and shaped) – I wouldn't develop that teaching system for another year. No, the audience simply looked at big blocks of text on a screen behind the stage, and I made them *memorise* my arrangement. It was as rock'n'roll as choir can get. I would sing each line of the song three ways, and the audience would repeat it back to me in their three harmonies as best as they could. And the song they were trying to memorise at this perfect show? 'Zombie' by The Cranberries.

The thing is, twenty-four days before this flawless gig, Dolores O'Riordan, the lead singer of The Cranberries, had died. Her death sent sad shockwaves around the world. Before the news reached me, however, I was already working on an arrangement of 'Zombie' for my next show. It was a strange, magical coincidence. I wondered if it would seem inconsiderate to sing her song after her death, but my years as a funeral singer had taught me that music can unlock some deep, unspeakable feelings. And we wouldn't be singing in a church – 500 of us would be belting her music into the night sky, and there would be beer, harmony and camaraderie. (In the event of my untimely death, please know I can't imagine anything more beautiful.)

The publisher's approval came through a few days before the show: I had permission to teach the song. I knew I'd been given the opportunity to make something special. I'm the first to admit that sometimes I fumble my song arrangements – I imagine incorrectly what will feel good for the audience and I only find out this miscalculation during the show (which always makes for a long night). But at this show, I got my arrangement right. The voices were cascading in, the harmonies were overlapping and swirling around each other, and I managed to explain it to the audience using just the right words.

It helped that everybody in the crowd sensed the importance of the music we were embodying. Nobody heckled. There wasn't even a whiff of mischief in the audience. People were holding hands, searching for the right notes together. Waveney hit every guitar chord perfectly. I moved my arms and the crowd moved their arms. I didn't say anything to embarrass myself. I glided across that tiny stage and everywhere I pointed, the right note appeared in the air.

Just before the final take, Evyn whispered in my ear, 'It might look cool if people shine their phone lights as they sing.' I told the crowd they should try it if it felt right.

A photo from this perfect show was taken by my singularly brilliant photographer Jacob Morrison, who was standing directly behind me as the song came together for the final time. I'm facing away from the camera and towards the audience, who are twinkling their phone lights in the distance. In the foreground and in crisp focus, I'm conducting with my right arm outstretched and it's covered in goosebumps. I just knew.

I mixed the audio recording of the final performance as soon as I got home and sent it off to Paris. She edited the

THE EVENT HORIZON

footage in her iconic way that makes you feel like you were there, too. When she had the video ready, I posted it online with the caption:

500 strangers assembled at Pub Choir to say thanks and farewell to Dolores O'Riordan with this epic cover of Zombie, by The Cranberries. Grab a hanky and happy cry your way through this one.

SINGING IS FOR EVERYONE. Filmed by Paris Owen and Jacob Sosnowski (Sleepy Mountain Films)[2]

This video exploded online. It went 'viral' in the pre-pandemic sense of the word. The morning after posting it, I woke up and saw *1 million views*. It was shared on The Cranberries' own social media page. It was a huge nod of approval for our small tribute to this special person. Suddenly, tens of thousands of new people started following Pub Choir online. They asked when the next show was, desperate to buy a ticket.

Also at my perfect show was an important journalist, who wrote Pub Choir's first newspaper review. There I was in print, described as a 'petite package of enthusiasm'. The article was hugely positive. And so, the national broadcaster invited me for a live TV interview. It wasn't the kind

---

[2] Neither Paris nor I noticed the video was incorrectly dated. I mention it just in case you go looking for it after reading this, and wonder why my timeline is inaccurate.

of puff-piece chat they squeeze in for 20 seconds after the weather. No, my perfect show was an actual newsworthy segment. Then the video cracked 2 million views online. And still the momentum didn't stop. News sites around the world wrote articles about it and shared our performance. Venues in other cities and other countries were asking how they could book Pub Choir. And people in Brisbane lined up in the rain to get into the next show.

Honestly, it hasn't slowed down ever since.

I like to think I might have got there anyway – that word of mouth would have slowly spread around Brisbane and beyond. And that through hard work and perseverance, I'd be in the exact same place I am now, even if this magical night never happened.

What an egotistical bunch of bullshit that'd be, though!

This was my perfect show. I was uniquely ready for it and I facilitated the experience. But more than that, I was also lucky. In such a bittersweet way. Out of a sad circumstance – the loss of one of the greatest vocalists of a generation – came an analogue moment of real human connection.

And I was there, exactly on time.

LOST IN TRANSLATION

On a trip to Japan in 2023, Evyn and I booked a private tour in Tokyo for some sightseeing with a *real* local. We're always insufferable on holiday and see ourselves as better than tourists. Even though we are tourists. But we're not like *other* tourists. No enthusiastic bus sightseeing for us! Taking photos at a famous monument? We'd much rather a tired, jaded local show us a nice cemetery before introducing us to their favourite grocery store.

So we booked a private walking tour with Vivian, a local Japanese guide. She was going to take us to all the cool spots the tourists didn't know about. She sent me a text the night before to confirm the details of our tour. Here's how our conversation went:

Vivian: *I'll be out the front of the café at 9 am holding a purple umbrella.*

> **Me:** *Thanks Vivian! We'll see you tomorrow at 9 o'clock! My boyfriend has a red beard and I am Eurasian.*
>
> **Vivian:** *Nice to meet you, Eurasian, see you tomorrow!*

Sometimes, Evyn will intervene if he notices a chaotic situation unfolding (always of my own creation). He'll help me draft a confident message or email to try and stop something getting out of hand. 'Just tell them both "no"!' he'll shout out from the bathroom while I natter on about being accidentally double-booked for a gig. But on this occasion, he found it funny, and I couldn't find the heart or the words to explain myself. So the following day, the three of us visited the graveyards and 7-Elevens of Tokyo: Vivian, Evyn and Eurasian.

In my everyday life, I have such trouble knowing how to interject when I feel something getting lost in translation. When a radio host misheard my name, rather than embarrassing *him*, I just let him call me 'Ostrich' for the whole interview. Just so nobody felt awkward (I'm nobody).

Equally, I didn't want to seem difficult to the Zambian waiter from whom I ordered a milkshake. 'Just add ice cream and milk together,' I said, when he asked me to clarify what a milkshake actually was. Thirty minutes later and beaming with pride, he laid a tray before me and stood back to watch with his fingers interlaced in anticipation. On the tray was a cup of ice, a jug of cream and a bottle of milk. He'd brought me ice, cream and milk. I consumed it all, by the way, and thereafter shat myself into a new galaxy. Thank goodness I didn't come across as difficult!

In my offstage life, I avoid conflict and confrontation at all costs, and it's constantly getting me into trouble. To realise that I can comfortably course-correct Pub Choir audiences during my show has been a wonderful gift: to me, from me. What a delightful feeling it is to believe in myself! When I give an instruction to the crowd and they sing back something unexpected, I always tell them straight away. 'You've absolutely missed the mark there,' I'll say to a group of 800 men, with a grin on my face and without batting an eyelid. 'Thank you for your *very* creative suggestions,' I'll joke to 2000 women, who've sung 2000 different notes except the one I asked for.

I'm convinced that nobody at my show wants to be lied to. Who knows better that they've missed the note than the singers themselves. What's the point in saying: 'You sound so amazing, you're doing so well!' if everybody in the room knows for a fact that they did *not* sound amazing, and that they definitely aren't doing so well. The shared relief is palpable when I acknowledge a miss, don't make a big deal out of it and offer to help.

Onstage, I'm at my best when I'm telling everyone what to do. It's what they signed up for! My performance confidence comes naturally and I'm addicted to the freedom of not second-guessing myself for a couple of hours. It feels good to tell the audience the truth.

I just wish I could bring this self-assuredness into my offstage life.

Offstage, I feel at my worst when I'm telling anyone what to do. Which isn't ideal, given that I run a business and I'm the boss. (If you have no interest in the machinations of management, I release you from the task of finishing this chapter.)

Oh, it makes me nauseous to dwell on it too long: I'm the boss of a business. I adore arranging music and making stuff with others, but the corporate side of my work is a necessary evil that I endure so I may continue doing the things I like and am good at.

When you're at the top of the hierarchical structure, you can't escalate a problem to anybody else. If you have an emergency, or if somebody is behaving like an arsehole, it's your responsibility to figure out what to do next and then send your pronouncements back down the ladder. (And if you're the sort of person who enjoys professionally bossing other people around, and we've sat next to each other at a dinner party, I definitely complained about you to Evyn all the way home afterwards.) To me, managing others at work is a rotten task. I can barely manage myself. Nobody is born a business manager. I can't think of anything more insulting to say about somebody! Figuring out how to manage others is something you have to learn in real time; I'm not convinced you can be taught how.

In an outrageous contradiction to the previous sentence, when I've been invited to present at networking events about leadership and business-building, on multiple occasions I've said 'yes'. The fraudulence! I've delivered private, corporate versions of Pub Choir to huge organisations and powerful people around the country. While I always try my best, and though it usually works out, I often leave the stage convinced that any company would be better off spending their 'team-building and networking' budget on, I dunno, paying their employees more?

Don't you think everybody would feel more energised on Monday if, instead of sending them to that expensive weekend retreat with bland buffet meals and activities where everybody has to build structures out of toothpicks, you just gave everyone Friday off?

No presentation can teach you how to manage bad workplace culture in an hour.

But I could certainly diagnose the health of your workplace culture in an hour:

- If I present Pub Choir as a team-building activity to your business, and everyone in management stands up the back of the room and doesn't join in with the group: your workplace culture is unwell.
- If everybody gets sloppily drunk because the only benefit of being at your networking event is the free booze: your workplace culture is critically ill.
- Worst of all, if your junior lawyers boo during an Acknowledgement of Country at the start of the team-building day: you may as well throw your whole legal firm in the bin, because your workplace culture is pure trash (a fairly specific example, but I stand by it).

Also! Now that I'm off and ranting on the corporate world: I'm suspicious of women-only networking events. Yes, I'm for the sisterhood, and for community and strength in numbers. But *only* if these women-specific events don't preclude the attendees from *also* attending mixed networking events, where all the big bosses shake hands and do deals. Do *not* let your line manager send 'you and the girls' off to morning tea (that you have to organise yourselves) if you don't get invited to the headline event. *Especially* if you need a full face of glamour makeup and an uncomfortable frock to be taken seriously at such an event. That's just misogyny disguised in lipstick and heels. I once emceed a women's-only awards night where I overheard attendees talking about how long they had dieted to fit into their equality dresses. Unsurprisingly, everybody spoke over the speeches of the winners, and the night culminated with a bonus award for 'Male Ally of the Year'. I'm no great corporate mind, but let me categorically state: *Fuck! That!*

Sorry for the tangent, but I do feel better.

Anyway, I run a business. And it seems to be going quite well, which is a surprise, most of all to me. People ask me to share the secret of how I started with nothing and ended up with a globally successful show, but I assure you, it wasn't because I'm a cutthroat negotiator and visionary strategist. If anything, I've been too easygoing, extremely confrontation-avoidant, and I didn't confidently know the difference between 'net' and 'gross' profit for more years than I'm willing to admit. (Fine, it was five years.)

All my business output happens because I'm afraid of the consequences if I *don't* follow through. I worried my way to the top.

That's the secret! Spread the word at your next networking event! I feel calm and secure about my musical abilities onstage, but what makes me try so hard offstage is my fear of public shame and upsetting people. If there is a problem back of house, I won't sleep until I'm sure I've found a way to move on. It's not pretty and it's not restful, but it's true.

If you're interested in running a business and being your own boss (congratulations *and* commiserations in advance), please don't let me deter you. I'm extraordinarily uninterested in gatekeeping the corporate world. I desperately want more people to create things and share their ideas – I just wouldn't want you going in blind. I'm not comfortable offering serious advice to anybody, but I *am* trying to get better at honesty offstage. In the spirit of that, I'll admit that, besides 'worrying a lot', I've collected a few more bits of intel about running a business over the last eight years. So here you go:

10 average-at-best business lessons I've learned in difficult circumstances that *might* be applicable in other situations

1. Keep records. Even half-arsed ones will do. Write in a journal whenever you can be bothered (I do this most days). Send emails or texts after you meet other

people – even just to say thanks. It'll only take 20 seconds! Find any way to keep track of what you're doing. Not necessarily for the legal reasons (wouldn't hurt, though), but to keep a record of your work for *you*. When you're slogging over an idea every day, it's difficult to see the big picture. What a treat to give yourself: the gift of tracking your own progress. You'd be surprised how all the tiny things add up in the end!

2. When you don't communicate difficult workplace messages because you want to avoid resentment, resentment will breed regardless. It's better to tell the truth, I *promise*. You're not allowed to feel too bitter about a problem if you haven't mentioned it to anyone else. Turns out, nobody can read your mind. You just have to say the difficult thing out loud, otherwise wires will get crossed and people will get cross. I would know. Please note: before you launch into your difficult conversation, maybe re-read the first point about keeping records.

3. You need support from others. But here's the kicker: if you ask the wrong people for support, it will make your life much harder. The trick is finding the right people. I've learned that you can't go horribly wrong working with anybody who regularly and comfortably uses *all* these four phrases: *Thank you, I'm sorry, How can I help?* and *I need help*. It works best if you also use those phrases.

4. Do not 'reply all' by default. Down with professional group chats! Those 28 people don't need their day interrupted with you responding 'okay' to the email thread. Now we've all got to open nineteen email tabs and wade back through idiotic 'haha' replies, looking for the skerrick of actual information we need. This is troll behaviour! If you need to say something, direct it to whoever needs to hear it, and leave everybody else alone! Nobody wants to build a business with a timewaster.

5. Following on from the previous point, ask yourself: could this online meeting/phone call/catch-up be replaced with a succinct email? Or are you thinking out loud and making other people watch? This is nobody's kink. I think it's marvellously respectful to give others the opportunity to digest important information in their own time so they can respond thoughtfully.

6. 'Difficult' and 'impossible' are two different things.

7. Pay people generously for their time. Time is the most finite resource in anyone's life. You can *probably* find more money. But you *definitely* can't find more time. I didn't take a regular wage for the first five years of Pub Choir and saved most of what I earned to be confident I could pay everybody else generously for their time. I'm sure the amount of effort most people put into their work reflects how much they feel their time has been valued (see points 3 to 5).

8. Controversial: exposure is not a currency – until it is. Mostly, people who ask me to work for free end up treating me as though I'm worthless, which I can't really complain about because the signs were there. However, *very rarely* the right exposure can change your life. Choose your moments wisely.

9. If you're the boss of anything, or anyone, be prepared to claim responsibility for *everything* that goes wrong. Even if it wasn't your fault – it was. Apologise. It will be okay. Ultimately, if you said you were in charge, everything comes back to you. This doesn't mean everybody can get away with bad behaviour; it just means you must also suffer the consequences. Are you ready to grovel for forgiveness for something that was out of your control? (Apparently, this doesn't apply to political leaders, but I think it should apply to them most of all.)

10. You *are* good enough to make something. Sorry to get weirdly earnest, but I mean it. I don't know if you're good enough to make a 'great' something, but everybody is capable of *starting* something. Time will pass by regardless, so you might as well give your idea a crack. I've been trying my best for eight years and, over time, it's worked out more often than it hasn't. And I can be a real idiot sometimes! Just try your best, even if your best is a bit rubbish. You won't ever get closer to your destination if you don't start at all.

So that's it! My ten underwhelming pieces of corporate advice. And if none of that advice helps, give worrying another go.

As for me, I'm determined to keep my head above the business waters.

All the anxiety I channel into managing everything I loathe doing lets me do the one thing I *should* be doing: standing onstage, convincing people to feel marginally less ashamed of their voice. I'm *sure* I'm supposed to be planting a seed of musical desire and creativity in others. And I tell you what: I'd drink another bottle of cream if it helped me do it. And I'm lactose intolerant.

IT'S COMPLIMENTARY

It's 2024 and my first show in Dallas, Texas. The moment I'd taken my bow and exited the stage, I ran as fast as possible to the merch desk so I could beat the audience there. When I bring Pub Choir to a new location for the first time, I like to look into people's faces as they leave the show to get a general sense of how they received my insane music lesson.

Did they like it?
Did I read their sense of humour right?
Was I too mean?
Are they happy?
Should I come back to this city?

It's a most neurotic ritual, which I feel at this point shouldn't come as a surprise to read.

As the crowd trickled out of the Dallas Theatre past the trestle table of T-shirts, participation ribbons and me drenched in sweat, I parroted out friendly statements at anybody who made eye contact. 'Thank you so much for coming!' and 'I hope to sing with you again!' I yelled, absolutely fishing for a compliment. In return, some people asked me for a photo, or to sign something, or to explain how the show came to be. I soak it all up as much as I can. I want to experience the audience up close – even just once in every city – for a small insight into how they feel, talk and behave.

Sometimes people disclose sad and intense things at the merch desk, like that their brother died that very morning, or they've recently been diagnosed with a terminal illness. Sometimes I'm on the receiving end of joyful news, like the grandmother who skipped over to me and said, 'Your show tonight was the happiest experience of my life . . . and my grandchild was born last week! Please don't tell my family!' (They won't be able to recognise you from that, will they?) Occasionally, I'll have a mystical exchange (my favourite), like the woman in San Francisco who held my hands, came very close to my face and whispered, 'I have a shrine to you in my house.'

'Oh!!!' I said. 'What do you mean by that?!'

To which she slyly replied, 'You *know* what I mean . . .'

In Dallas, a woman in a tie-dyed, flowy dress with a long, grey plait draped over her shoulder made a beeline towards me. Without warning, her hands were around my waist and her head was tilted back a little to 'take me all in' – like she was at a restaurant, had forgotten her glasses and I was the menu she was trying to read at arm's length.

IT'S COMPLIMENTARY

'You're even more beautiful up close,' she said in her friendly drawl.

'Haha, I'm glad, I guess!' I giggled unsurely, acutely aware of her hands touching a soft part of my body.

She smiled with her eyes, nose and whole face, in that crinkly way I love. She squeezed my waist firmer still. 'I just mean, I've watched so many of your videos on YouTube and you're runnin' about all over the place in those. But up close, to see you in action in person . . . you're a darn supermodel!'

Aloud, I responded, 'Aw, that's so nice of you to say. Thank you!' I've learned to always say 'thank you' to somebody who has plucked up the courage to come over and express their support. But inside I thought, *This woman is deranged and has me confused for somebody else.*

I have lived the majority of my life certain that I am an ugly person. My psychologist likes to call this 'body dysmorphia', but I like to call it 'just a thing about myself that I've spent a lot of time worrying about but am trying to learn to be less bothered by as I get older'. Admittedly, her name for it is catchier.

To put it another way: 'beautiful' is a powerful card to play in life, but I don't think it's my best option. I'm going for 'clever'. I will destroy you in a game of Scrabble. I arrange songs in my head and run a business or . . . whatever it is I do (I'm not always sure). I'm convinced that my most valuable social currency is invisible – impossible for others to know at a glance – and I'm trying to be fine with this. I want to get myself to a place, not where I look in the mirror and say,

'I'm beautiful! I'm perfect!' but where I can genuinely say, 'Is there anything in my teeth, and does it matter?'

Currently, I'm nowhere near this point. In the way I hear alcoholics talk about how many days, weeks or years they've been sober, I too am taking my recovery from bulimia one day at a time. I haven't had a forced spew since 2016. But the desire to stick my fingers down my throat lives so very close to the surface – only a few knuckles deep. Honestly, it would feel like such a relief to give in to my urge to purge that I'm sure if I made myself vomit even once more, I would never stop.

I don't know how any millennial girl entered adulthood *without* an eating disorder. Our collective body image really went through it in the 2000s. I'm proud of us as a cohort, disordered eating or not, because we had to be tough to make it through those 'nothing tastes as good as skinny feels' years.

People occasionally call me ugly online, but they aren't the source of my insecurities. In fact, nobody has ever said it to my face outright. Perhaps the closest I've come was in 2012, when my then-band Astrid & the Asteroids was flown to Sydney to meet a famous music agent as part of a prestigious award I won for my songwriting. He said my music was 'okay', but compared with more successful female artists my age, the obvious difference was that '*they* clearly exercise and take care of their appearance'. This pasty, limp-handshake-of-a-man's advice for my original music was for me to 'look better'. But still, it wasn't him who did it.

IT'S COMPLIMENTARY

No, as a straight woman, my ugliness worries developed through the adolescent absence of male attention (cue the sound of a collective sigh from feminists everywhere, me included). During elaborate games of catch-and-kiss played at primary school, no one was ever chasing me. And let me tell you, I was running *slowly*. In high school, boys would froth over my friends and finger them on the bleachers. Have you ever seen the fingernails of a teenage boy? I didn't want any of those talons touching me, no thank you. Then again, none of them offered. I couldn't ignore the fact that I wasn't appealing to even the world's horniest, most desperate demographic: Year 9 boys.

I remember expressing a more PG-rated version of my woes to my dad in the car on the way to school. He was a teacher at my high school, so knew the lay of the land.

'All the other girls are so . . . blonde. And skinny. And I just feel so uncool, and like I'm on the outside looking in at everybody else having fun.'

Like all significant conversations that happen in a car, my dad kept looking straight ahead at the road with two hands on the wheel. 'All of us have many seasons in life,' he said. 'And some girls in your class are living the best season of their life right now, while they're at school. Just let them. Your best season is coming later on and, trust me, it's better to wait.'

So, I focused on being funny, smart and proactively mean, and I got through fine enough. (I'm very sorry if you experienced my mean years. I still shudder to remember how I behaved when I was thirteen.) In my senior year, my peers voted me school captain. Maybe my 'ugly and smart' season was workable and fine!

But then I lost weight and everything changed.

After graduating, I spent those two months in Zambia, and came back to Australia as a physically smaller person. I'd spent the trip eating almost nothing but maize and fresh guava, while walking, fasting and praying on my knees every day. I'd also contracted malaria. Pretty different from my sedentary lifestyle back at home where I'd eat four (4) grilled cheese sandwiches on the daily as my after-school/before-dinner snack, for which I used puff pastry instead of bread (delicious, no regrets). So, yeah, I lost a lot of weight in Zambia.

When I returned to Australia, for the first time *ever* in my life, people said nice things about the way I looked.

I remember seeing two girls from school at the shops, elbowing each other before waving me over in shock. 'You've lost so much weight. You look *SO much prettier!*' they assured me. When I went to see if I could get my bakery job back, my boss told me she'd gladly have 'such a lovely figure back behind the counter'! Friends and acquaintances agreed that I looked so beautiful – now. The most telling response was that nobody in my family said anything about my fairly dramatic weight loss. Usually such chatty, unfiltered people, I knew that when they go quiet, words are sitting wedged in their throats unexpressed.

I had the same face, the same personality, the same fashion sense, but there was less of me. The world around me told me that I was no longer ugly. I was beautiful now! I put it all together. I had previously assumed that I'd never be called pretty and that I couldn't do anything about it. Turns out, I just needed to be thinner! To go from being the ignored chubby-funny friend to being told 'you look stunning!' is a significant confidence leap when you're sixteen years old. And it's a simple fact that society is nicer to thin people (and unless you've been both fat and thin, I will not be accepting your feedback on the subject at this time).

It felt *amazing* for people to say nice things about how I looked. I treasured everybody's compliments. And I let them settle so deeply into my soul they made me sick – literally.

Filled with a dread that I would return to my past self, where nobody said nice things about my appearance, I freaked out. I didn't want to find any of the weight I'd lost because then I'd go back to being invisible/way more visible. So I put my fingers down my throat and made myself sick after every meal for eight years until my hair started falling out and I had ulcers in my mouth and my vision went blurry whenever I stood up and everything smelled like vomit. (These are not beauty tips: I wish to be an example to nobody.)

With Evyn's help, I eventually stopped doing this brutal thing to myself. When I finally confessed to him what was going on, it's the only time in our now seventeen-year relationship I've seen him properly cry. He was so compassionate and non-judgemental, and never made me feel stupid for being unwell. Honestly, I think his approach could solve a lot of the world's problems.

I explained to him that I could no longer trust the signals my body gave me. 'I can't tell the difference between starving and full. They feel the same. And when I eat even the smallest bite, it's like this switch is flipped in my brain, like I've passed the point of no return.'

'What's the point of no return?'

'It's like . . . my consciousness leaving my body. Almost like I'm watching myself from above. Suddenly, I've opened the door of the fridge or the cupboard, and I'm eating as much as I possibly can, as fast as I can. Then it feels like I wake up and I realise what I've done and I make myself sick again and again until it's all gone.'

He gave me a long, squeezy, sniffly hug. Then he asked, 'Would it help if we ate together?'

Evyn offered to accompany me through mealtimes. 'I trust my hunger cues a lot' he told me. 'When I'm hungry, it's because I need food. When I'm full, it's because I've had enough. Let's eat together, and I'll let you know how I'm feeling as we go.'

Evyn is a thin person, so I believed him. I'd try to match him as he took each mouthful of food. When he said he was full, I would stop, too. He never commented on how much I had eaten (very important), only on how he felt. Then we'd sit together and talk about TV shows and our university assignments until the threat had passed. When we weren't physically in the same place, I'd call him and he would stay on the phone until I had eaten and felt safe in my body again.

2022: Astrid high-kicking on stage in Hobart, Australia. *Photo: Jacob Morrison*

2023: Pub Choir performs at the Australian Embassy in Washington, DC. (*L–R*: Hugh, Paris, Astrid, Evyn, the Hon. Kevin Rudd, Dana, John).

2024: Astrid and Evyn sit together backstage at Brisbane's Riverstage.
Photo: Kristina Wild

2023: Astrid conducting onstage with legendary trumpeter, John Hoffman, in Brisbane. *Photo: Jacob Morrison*

2024: Pub Choir® raises $147,000 for Women's Legal Service Queensland at Brisbane's Riverstage. (*L–R*: Madison, David, Astrid, Sahara). *Photo: Jacob Morrison*

2024: Astrid is a guest on the TV show *Spicks & Specks*. (*L–R*: Alan Brough, Astrid Jorgensen, Zoë Coombs Marr, Adam Hills, Anthony Albanese, Myf Warhurst, Ben Lee). *Photo courtesy of the ABC*

2024: A selfie of Pub Choir's® tour crew in Scotland. (*L–R*: Astrid, Paris, Sahara, Evyn, John).

2024: Astrid preparing backstage in Brisbane. *Photo: Kristina Wild*

2024: Astrid receives her Medal of the Order of Australia from Queensland Governor, Her Excellency the Hon. Dr Jeannette Young AC PSM.
Photo: Courtesy of Government House Queensland

IT'S COMPLIMENTARY

It was not linear progress. But after a good few years of love and patience (plus a great doctor who tracked my internal health), my body started to give me signals that I wanted to listen to. I learned to trust my hunger again. If you are battling a disordered relationship with eating, it *is* possible to feel better. (I want that so much for you and I promise you haven't done anything wrong.)

But also – and this is what I really wanted to say in this chapter – *that's* why I don't want to get Botox. I know I took an indirect route to suddenly arrive at this point with no warning, but the thing is, I no longer want to hurt myself for the singular goal of changing how I look, so other people think I'm beautiful 'now'.

Our bodies are sacks of meat and blood and other stuff that house all our inside bits. (Evyn is the doctor, not me.) Our body is our home. The relationship we have with our body is the longest relationship we will ever have. And this might seem obvious, but I've discovered that when I don't abuse my body/home, I'm a much happier, higher-functioning person. And I have truly explored the alternative! Yes, the most compliments I've ever received about how my meat-sack looked was when I was being downright cruel to myself. So, no, I don't always feel comfortable when people give me compliments about my appearance. I appreciate it comes from a supportive place, and that 'beautiful' can be a code for other complimentary words like 'intelligent' or 'confident', but that's difficult to know unless they are the words we actually say.

If you have Botox and/or fillers, I'm sure you look smooth, shiny, young and well-rested. I love that for you! Alternatively, if your smile crumples and wrinkles your whole face, I probably save my best stories to tell you, simply for the excellent facial responses I'll get in return. I love that for me (selfish). But your face has nothing to do with my face. I want to find a way to feel neutral about my face. To stop worrying if it's ugly or beautiful, and instead find out what my face was destined for. I have no other life to find out! I'm curious to see what happens next to my eyelids and that cluster of freckles on my left cheek.

Do I wear makeup? Absolutely slap the stuff on. Did I pay for invisible braces as an adult? With mountains of cash! Do I get my eyebrows done? By a *tattooist*! How is that better than Botox? It's not! So why do I do it? Well, I'm certainly not doing it for me. Not a chance! I won't pretend that I pay somebody to stick ink and needles into my eyebrows because it feels nice. Ha!

Do we do any of it for ourselves, *really?*

If you were the last person left on an apocalyptic, scorched world (a proper fantasy of mine), do you *really* think you'd wax, pluck, rip, laser, peel, inject, thread, exfoliate, lift, pummel, needle, scrape or whiten any part of yourself to *feel beautiful*? Sweet Lucifer knows I would not. I'd grow all the hair on my body from head to toe, and combine every strand into one practical, greasy, mega-braid. Unburned of the worry of maintaining my weight, I'd methodically

IT'S COMPLIMENTARY

raid each grocery store and attempt to eat all the food in the world. And that'd just be Week 1. I'd permanently renounce all denim; instead, I'd wear soft bedsheets with head-hole cut-outs, in colours that do absolutely nothing for my complexion. I'd abandon my futile five-step skincare regime, and with all that extra time I'd track down every shapewear factory on earth and burn them to the ground. I would never, under any circumstance, wear heavy dangly earrings or bleach my butthole because it felt nice. Note: I would still wear a sensible bra because a sore back is no joke, apocalypse or not.

In the real world, I put on my itchy stockings and strap myself into my expensive, fitted and unbreathable costumes. I preen my hair and primp my face, then I walk onstage for everybody to look at me, feeling as if I'm walking into battle. Ideally, you'll think I look like the sort of person who's allowed to charge money for tickets to a show. I'll be hoping I've done enough to my appearance to convince you to stay and hear what I have to say.

I *know* how much nicer people can be when you look a certain way. I'm trying to game the system, too. I'm a hypocrite with one foot on the slippery slope of the beauty industry and the other on a banana peel, trying to stand my ground in any way I can. I can't tumble all the way down that mountain again. Anyway, I haven't got the right shoes on to climb back up. (I'm wearing uncomfortable boots with a heel so my calves look more defined.) Botox is where I'm drawing one wrinkly, fine line for myself. Does that count for anything?

It counts to me. I'm a complex, imperfect, insecure person, hoping my best season is still to come. I want to recognise her when she arrives.

15 REASONS I MIGHT NOT SLEEP TONIGHT

1. I've spent the past two hours holding a bright piece of glass close to my face, which contains all the knowledge *and* idiocy of humanity. This is a bad way to relax before bed. I am aware of it, but I'll continue to have my little phone scroll before I try to sleep because I am weak. And I like the jokes and dog videos.

2. I opened up the comments section on one of my social media posts, and somebody said something cruel but clever about me. For example, the YouTube commenter who wrote, 'She has a face like a horse that you'd feed by smashing apples through a tennis racquet.' It's an incredibly specific and imaginative insult. I know it's rude and I hate it but . . . I also respect it. I can't stop thinking about it. What does it *mean*?

3. I've just announced what song I'm going to teach at the next Pub Choir show and people are throwing about

the D-word. 'That song is *disappointing*. Yuck, we don't want to come anymore!' I try to remind everybody that the song isn't the focus of the show – the goal is to make art together and be kind to each other. And that it's impossible to find a song that is everyone's favourite. But I'm wasting my breath. Once I've announced the song, I lie awake in bed, crushed under the weight of three ladies' disappointment, and the twelve people who've asked for refunds because they hate the song. (I promise I'd ignore them and focus on the avalanche of positive comments IF I KNEW HOW. SOMEBODY TELL ME HOW.)

4. I'm on tour and am jet-lagged, dehydrated, malnourished, confused, delirious, overstimulated and uncomfortable. I do not know the day, time or name of the city I'm in. As a childfree person, the phrase 'my child is overtired' had previously mystified me. When hearing parents use it to explain why their kid wasn't sleeping, I'd thought smugly to myself, *If your child was tired, they'd fall asleep.* But touring has taught me that you can, in fact, be too tired to sleep. I am the child.

5. I'm remembering the time I asked somebody to house-sit for me while I was away, and I'd accidentally left my poo journal open on the counter for them to discover. Like almost every woman I know, my digestive system is out to get me. It hurts, confuses and betrays me, and I don't know why. So I once briefly tried to record my bowel movements

15 REASONS I MIGHT NOT SLEEP TONIGHT

in a peace-brokering effort to understand them. In this journal, I had timestamped my poos, given descriptions and artist renditions of their appearance, and discussed in great detail how much effort I had put into their creation. And then I left this book sitting open for my house-sitter to find. It was closed and put away when I returned home from my trip. I think about this a lot.

6. I have an early-morning start. Is this the world's most powerful brain stimulant? Simply knowing that I must wake up earlier than normal ensures that I won't sleep at all. I can forget about having any REM if my alarm is set for 4 hours from now. Make that 3 hours 55 minutes. Should I check the time again just in case I've slipped into a coma, been asleep for nine days and accidentally missed my flight? Oh. I still have 3 hours 55 minutes to sleep. 3 hours 54 minutes. Shit!

7. I'm on tour and am being driven mad wondering if I have the right crew configuration. I want you to consider for one moment all the people you've ever worked with. How many of them would you also like to live with? Really, I've only ever met one person in my whole life that I wanted to live with and, even then, it can be touch-and-go.

    It is unnatural, unpleasant and unreasonable to see your colleagues 24/7 for months, and *not* feel something deep in your soul. Your polished, professional self can be very different from the person you become when you're angry and hungry. Touring exposes the primal animal living inside you that you desperately try to hide from others. But it'll come out on tour. We'll see your inner gremlin. Not everybody feels equally at ease in this exposed environment, so I feel extraordinarily lucky to have found a touring crew that gels. Our inner gremlins get along. It just took me a lot of sleepless nights to get there.

8. The general state of the world. You *know*. All this *gestures vaguely*. Once in a radio interview. I was asked what one thing I would do to make the world a better place. 'I'd force everybody to learn the difference between "opinions" and "facts",' I said. I hope *somebody* out there knows the difference between those two things. I'm doubtful about some of the power-hungry idiots who are in charge, but hey, that's just my opinion. Somebody will *probably* do something about climate change, won't they? And war, racism, violence, loneliness, poverty . . . bloody hell, what are we gonna *do* about everything?

9. I've written a song in my sleep. Sometimes I dream in music, and occasionally this dream music is so vivid that it wakes me up. I dazedly scramble out of the room to try and record this subconscious song on my phone before it slips out of my remembering. Usually, I've forgotten it almost instantaneously and find myself in the corridor, blinking and confused, wondering why I'm standing there at 2.30 am.

One night, however, I sat bolt upright in bed. As Evyn sleepily asked, 'whasappening?' I was already halfway out the bedroom door.

'I've written an incredible song in my sleep. My best *ever!*' I called back. I mumble-recorded my surefire award-winning song idea into my phone. Satisfied I'd captured it, I came back to bed.

'Didyagetit?' Evyn yawned as I crawled back under the covers.

'Yes! Yesssss. It's an absolute winner!' I whispered, kicking my little feet under the sheets in excitement.

The next morning over coffee, Evyn asked me to play it. 'Come on then, what's this hit song?'

With butterflies in my stomach, I took out my phone and pressed 'play' on the recording. We listened. It was the sound of me slurring my way through Lionel Richie's hugely famous tune, 'All Night Long'. I really thought I had something there.

10. I'm in a hotel where there is no intermediate bedsheet between the fitted sheet on the mattress and the outer blanket. My skin is touching the skin of 10,000 others who have sweated and shed under this same blanket. Make middle sheets great again!

11. I have an upcoming show, and the weather forecast is predicting rain. Even though I don't control the weather, the number of complaints that come my way if it rains on a Pub Choir show day is – to me – diabolical.

I can't cancel outdoor shows simply because of the weather – the outdoors is where weather *always* happens and venues make you sign a contract to this effect. And I swear on all that is sacred to me, there is one person in this world who wants good weather on Pub Choir's show day more than anybody else: me. I am lying in my bed, wide awake, refreshing the meteorology forecast on my phone, *praying for sun*.

12. It's just a bit too hot.

13. I'm wondering if I'm supposed to have children. I don't want to. Is that allowed? I can't believe everybody else just . . . dives in to such a monumental task. The biggest, bravest task of all! Women are so tough – other women, that is. Not me. I have never for one moment envisaged holding a baby of my own. I simply don't want a baby coming out of my body; it does *not* look fun. And it's so risky! I did a questionnaire with a financial adviser and he said that, in his whole career, he'd never met a more risk-averse client. I felt so proud of myself! I hate gambling!

    I swear, I'm not some mean old crone. I actually love kids. I've just never thought to myself, *Gee, I wish I could grow some kids who could live in my house forever because it's too quiet here*. On several occasions, I've been told by a parent: 'You don't know what love is until you've had a child of your own.' (This is categorically rude, so scrub that from your bank of small-talk phrases if it's in there.) If anything, I feel like I know love so well, I am content. I'm full! Don't need another bite, thank you!

But I *will* smile at your baby on the bus. Can I hold your baby? Maybe my maternal instinct will kick in soon. I guess you never know. I'll think on it some more tonight.

14. I'm imagining how my perfect, horrid, cute, misbehaving, intelligent, adorable, angry little dog Penny will die one day. Even on my most wretched, undeserving days, she is ecstatic to see me. She twirls in happy circles and cries with joy, even when I come back from the letterbox. I was only gone for ten seconds! So now I'm mourning the death of my dog, who is currently in perfect health and entirely impervious to my sadness. But oh, what will I do when it happens?

15. I'm trying to process the fact that, when I look up at the night sky, I'm not actually looking *up* but *out*. We live on a giant floating ball. We're never really looking up; we're looking outwards towards an infinite universe. As I lie in bed, gravity is pulling me towards the core of the planet. But in the other direction? Away from the planet? You could look outwards forever. It makes me feel very small and insignificant, and sometimes, in the end, that does help me get to sleep.

OLD DOG, NEW TRICKS

'm sitting at my computer, autotuning the howls of dogs. For money. I've already finished lining up twenty different dogs barking so that their woofs happen in time with the music, and if I can just find one more dog howl, I can send off this audio and get paid. I scroll through all the video files to check once more. Not one more howl to be found! I'll have to message my manager John about his dog Todd:

> ***Me:*** *Does Todd howl on demand?*

John: *Todd has no control over anything he does.*

> ***Me:*** *I just need one long howl and then I'd be finished*

John: *One time Todd howled when I played the piano? I'll try it and get back to you.*

It is September of 2020. I haven't left my house in months. I have no job. But in a surprising twist, a pet clothing company has offered to pay me a significant stack of money if I can figure out how to turn the sound of dogs barking into music. But to make sense of 'Pup Choir' (for dogs), I need to go back eighteen months.

All the way back to Gerry.

I'm not sure Pub Choir (for humans) would have ventured to the United States if it wasn't for the saintly intervention of one Gerald Gorman. An Australian expat living in New York, Gerry attended a 2019 Pub Choir show in Melbourne while on holiday visiting his family. This lovely, clever man who was a total stranger – just *some guy* – enjoyed my show so much that he sent me this unassuming, unbelievable email:

> *Astrid, I visited Melbourne in March and my brother took twelve of us to your show. It was the best fun I have had in a long time :-) I live in New York and have some friends who do music events/own venues. Any chance we can get Pub Choir in NYC? I'd donate $10k and make introductions if you wanted . . . I don't have any business interest but would be happy to be a catalyst for bringing a fun activity to New York and helping promote Australian talent.*

Naturally, I figured this was some kind of trap. Until I googled him. I had never talked with the CEO of a big company, let alone somebody with $10,000 to spare. I responded with something aloof and understated like: 'ABSOLUTELY YES PLEASE THANK YOU'. Suddenly, we were having phone calls and discussing marketing strategies. Gerry would send no-frills emails with subjects like 'Next Steps' and I would draft flowery replies then scrub out every auxiliary word before pressing 'send', so I could pretend to be as capable as Gerry imagined me to be.

Gerry:
How many in your crew? I am talking to a senior consulate official re assistance for your visa. They've sent through questions: put succinct answers under each.
Regards,
Gerry

Me:
Gerry!!!! ~~Absolutely heroic,~~ thanks ~~for the update~~.
~~I've popped my~~ answers below. ~~I hope they are ok, let me know if not.~~
Astrid

Everything moved at the speed of Gerry (fast). Four months after his first email, Pub Choir was in the USA for a mini-run of shows that were only mildly cursed (high praise when describing a tour). I sold out two shows in New York City, a place I'd never been before, and the audiences there were just as excited as those in Australia. I felt a shift in my understanding of myself. I reluctantly accepted that

I'm good at convincing people to sing. Fine! I admit it! Every person at those NYC gigs was a stranger to me and I was bossing them around and it was *working,* just like at home. I needed to change my approach a little bit (you can't tease Americans as freely as you can tease Australians), but I figured it out quickly and the audiences were phenomenally enthusiastic in response.

On this first US trip, I didn't want to waste my incredible Gerry-backed opportunity. My crew and I had come a long way for those NYC shows, so I asked John to book events in Los Angeles and San Francisco, too. Those Gerry-less shows were . . . not a success. Pub Choir's first gig in Los Angeles was in Skid Row, which we quickly learned was the name of an infamous neighbourhood, but also described our bodily response to being there. Stepping over a pregnant woman shooting a needle of something directly into her belly, so we could get inside our accommodation, was a clue that this was not the right location to host a whimsical singalong. I'll describe that show as 'rough' and leave it at that.

After Skid Row in LA, we had our Skid Show in San Francisco. While sitting backstage an hour before the doors opened, a terrifying stench started wafting through the venue. The manager asked to speak to me.

'Bad news. We're gonna have to cancel your show.'

'WHAT! Why on earth would you do that? We've flown across the world for this show!'

'Seriously? Can you not smell *that*?'

'What, that sour, rancid, farty, vomit, rotten egg smell? I was hoping that maybe . . . you'd just had a big lunch before we arrived?'

Alas. A sewage pipe directly below the venue had burst and an entire suburb's-worth of poo slurry was bubbling up through cracks in the stage floorboards. Obviously, this literal shit-show was cancelled, but I did manage to sing with some of the audience out the front of the venue. Then we all went to a bar afterwards and got magnificently drunk.

And that was Pub Choir's first trip to the USA. It was not boring. I wanted more.

For my second USA attempt, I tried to move fast. I had John book the same cities just four months later, and we attempted to rely less on Gerry (huge mistake). I managed to sell out the shows ahead of the tour . . . *before* I secured a work visa. File that under 'Things Done in the Wrong Order That Seem Obvious After the Fact'. I had to cancel the shows at the last minute, losing all the venue deposits and months of work.

That was Pub Choir's second interaction with the USA.

For my third act, I was determined to redeem myself. Given the debacle I created while trying to be self-sufficient, Gerry hopped onboard to help again. He paid a publicist, sponsored my work visa, and even went so far as to print out posters and put them up across NYC. (I need to send this man some flowers . . . does a book chapter count?) I finally had something to contribute on my end: Pub Choir had been booked as an artist for the South by Southwest festival in

Austin, Texas. To be included in the lineup of this prestigious, coveted, cool festival . . . for my dorky choir show? It felt like somebody had made a mistake and I needed to capitalise on the opportunity before I was found out. John booked a tour around Pub Choir's South By Southwest appearances. The visa came through *before* announcing the shows, which was definitely the correct order of doing things. Thank you, Gerry.

I brought a pared-back crew: just me, Paris (video), John (management) and Waveney (guitar). We headed to the USA for our third attempt at a Pub Choir tour.

In March 2020.

Bugger.

We didn't make it to Austin. South By Southwest was cancelled because of some sort of global health pandemic. I managed to perform one show in Los Angeles, but by the time we'd reached San Francisco, the rest of the tour had been axed by the venues themselves. What the heck would the four of us do in the USA for a fortnight with no shows? We sat on our total of two motel beds (you do the maths, it was grim) and smoked weed and laughed for hours in our horrible accommodation. *But what will we do tomorrow?*

Thankfully, the next day I received an important call from a mystery hero. The authoritative voice said, 'As a fan of your show, my *personal* advice to you and your team is to leave the country. Get to an airport, wait in any line for a flight and return to Australia as soon as you can.'

Once again, I'd flown to the USA to piss my (and Gerry's) money into the wind, but I knew the advice was correct:

we needed to get home. There were apocalyptic scenes in the USA during March 2020. And we four were sharing two beds in one room that smelled like bleach and I'm pretty sure had bed bugs. Paris had a weird cough (turned out not to be Covid, just poor lifestyle). Every shop and restaurant was closed.

'Let's go home, you guys,' I sighed.

The four of us piled into a rental van and drove seven hours to LAX airport – our best chance at getting on a standby list to fly home. There, I scrolled my phone, slack-jawed, as I watched the cancellation of every future Pub Choir show back in Australia. In twenty-four hours, 20,000 tickets disappeared while we sat waiting on the cold airport floor. But we *did* all get on the same flight back to Brisbane, for which I'm truly grateful. On that journey home, I discussed with my tour crew the idea of still singing with people, somehow.

'Think of all those people who wanted to sing with Pub Choir, now stuck at home.' I moaned to the others. 'There *must* be a way to virtually sing together. In fact . . .' I picked at the thread of a memory that had appeared in my brain. 'I remember this choir guy giving a TED Talk, maybe like ten years ago? His name is . . . Eric Whitacre? He made a virtual choir video where people weren't singing in the same room. Maybe we could do something like that?'

John pulled up the video on his phone. In 2009, American choral juggernaut Eric Whitacre had spotted a YouTube video of a singer beautifully performing the soprano line from his piece called 'Sleep'. He put a call out for other singers to join her. A year later, he unveiled a virtual choir with 243 individual videos collated into one performance. It had expensive-looking graphics and required musically literate participation from the singers, but the idea of stitching individual performances together was *very* cool.

'Surely we could think of a DIY version of this that's more accessible?' asked John.

I agreed. 'I'd want to keep the same Pub Choir kinda energy for sure. No entry barriers or sheet music to participate, and just let people sing along with my arrangements as averagely as they want. But,' I paused, 'the challenge would be figuring out how the hell to sync all the performances into one video . . .'

John, Waveney and I looked across to Paris, whose job it would be to figure that part out.

'Well . . .' she said, 'I have no idea how to make a virtual choir, but . . . I could try?'

'That's my girl!!' I said. At the exact same time, John said 'That's my boy!!' We all laughed. Paris was ready to continue our adventure.

As is always my inclination, I decided to place unnecessary public pressure on myself by releasing a statement on social media. I posted online, explaining that Pub Choir's US tour had been cancelled due to the Covid-19 pandemic, and added this little teaser at the end:

We are intensely optimistic as people and we know
we will sing again with you in the future! We are also
currently plotting a way to still sing with you and will be

doing a live announcement on Facebook soon. I mean . . . if there are so many people sitting at home in isolation, it seems like a great time to sing. Stand by 😊

Now we had to follow through. And sure enough, by the time we'd landed back in Australia, the plan was ready. I called it 'Couch Choir'.

Couch Choir ran on the same principles as Pub Choir: ordinary people sharing their voices as best they can. But rather than me teaching a live audience, I prerecorded my instructions. I recorded myself playing the piano, then Waveney added guitar over the top to make a backing track. I wrote three vocal harmonies and sang them myself as three separate, solo performances. Paris filmed me mouthing along. I decided to move my hands up and down to help people at home follow where the notes were going – kind of like a living PowerPoint presentation. John built a website and posted the three instructional videos for people to watch and learn. Then Waveney and I went live on social media to invite people to participate.

'There are three videos of me singing different harmonies, and I want you to choose the one that suits you the best,' I said. 'Listen to that video on repeat until you can sing along with me and then . . . record a video of yourself singing along with me!'

'Don't stress too much about what you look like, or what you sound like, or if you've made a mistake,' Waveney said warmly down the camera to the live online audience.

'Yeah, don't overthink it. Just send your video as soon as you're done, and we'll edit you into one mega, virtual video,' I added (and by 'we', I meant 'Paris').

By now, I'm sure you've all seen examples of virtual choirs because they became fairly commonplace during the Covid years, but in March 2020, I believe Couch Choir pioneered an accessible way of singing online, together (sort of).

Absolutely everybody was welcome to participate. I never charged anybody one cent to access the materials. It seemed like a nice thing to do, and also, who can be bothered shaking down somebody online for $5? Not me. I wasn't even sure anybody would be interested, because it's a hugely courageous act: to send your singing voice to strangers online and trust that they won't betray you.

In three days, just over 1000 people sent in videos from all around the world. For days, John, Paris and I sat with our laptops overheating, watching every single video submission and sorting them into different voice parts. Paris synced up the visuals of the videos and, with the help of Jacob Sosnowski, they included *every single submission* into one mega choral performance. The enormous grids they devised, along with the beautiful sweeping features of individual performances, made me weep. Paris's video editing was a work of art.

I extracted the audio from every video, and evened out their volumes and timings so every voice could be heard (not heard) equally. Paris and I did everything we could to leave nobody behind. The diversity of the participants was amazing to me. We had singers from every continent (except

Antarctica, boo). People were sending in videos from their cars, apartments, farms, mountaintops and even houseboats in the middle of the ocean.

I posted the first Couch Choir video online and it went nuts. It was delivered directly to the screens of everybody stuck at home, who were feeling disconnected and scared for their future. Those 1000 strangers had sung averagely and individually, but the collective beauty of all those voices showed the world that our shared humanity was more powerful than our separateness. It seemed as if it was the first bit of good news since the beginning of the Covid pandemic. So much so that the BBC World Service asked if they could use a clip to close their bulletins.

For the second Couch Choir session, 6000 people submitted a video. Our laptops crashed every minute and my internet couldn't cope. A whip-smart friend from school, Jodie Pattinson, helped get Paris, John and me into a dormant university computer lab to use their editing software, and download what felt like the entire internet as we churned through the huge amount of submissions. In that same week, I must have been interviewed by every media outlet in the world. Online participants started sending donations to thank us for giving them something positive to do in lockdown. We'd done a nice thing, and everybody was being kind in return (which is not how these things usually work out).

By the third Couch Choir session, a kind man in tech named Terry Weber donated two hardcore laptops, two huge hard drives, and a fuck-off computer monitor to help beef up Couch Choir's production. (Here's to the Gerrys, Terrys and Jodies of this world!) I found a sound engineer, Steve Thornely, to take over the audio mixing of thousands of voices, which had now far surpassed my technical capabilities. The workflow was down pat. As a team, we pumped out eleven Couch Choir sessions in total, featuring more than 21,000 individual video submissions.

During the longest stretch of time in history that human beings hadn't sung together, Pub Choir's social media following doubled. Mariah Carey tweeted about it. Businesses sent emails from all around the world with event budgets they needed to 'circle back' on, and a work-from-home team they didn't know how to connect. They asked me to facilitate private Couch Choir sessions for the corporate world. Suddenly, I could pay my crew properly. Even though singing together in rooms was illegal, Couch Choir kept singing alive. And it was all possible because we gave our time and talents freely to our community, with no expectation of reward.

AN ASIDE: Stop! Don't ask artists to work for free. That is not the moral of this story. The thing that happened here was an *anomaly* because the world was very weird at the time. 'Exposure' is terrible currency. You should pay people real money for their work, okay? Art has value beyond being purely a distraction or entertainment. If you want trained professionals to entertain

you at your event, hand over the cash and nobody gets hurt.

The things I saw in Couch Choir videos constantly surprised me, or made me emotional. John, Paris and I sat around for days at a time, scouring through the thousands of videos and sharing the zaniest things we'd seen.

'LOOK! Here's a man singing while pole dancing!' John shouted. We crowded around his screen and whooped with excitement.

Five minutes later: 'GET A LOAD OF THIS! Here's an entire, all-female ju-jitsu studio high-kicking and singing!' announced Paris. We gawked at the screen and I felt a little welling of emotion in my eyes seeing all those amazing, tough girls and women singing together.

Ten minutes later: 'Hold on. Is this . . . is this bloody KEVIN RUDD?' I yell at the top of my lungs. The friggin' former prime minister of Australia submitted a video of himself singing, just like everybody else, and didn't even draw our attention to it. (Lucky that we genuinely did watch everything.)

Up close, most of the voices were average – at best. But together, they sounded electrifying. The singing was the same quality as at Pub Choir's live show (variable), but each person had spent time with their own voice, accepted it and sent their recording to me anyway. And unlike the shared euphoria and anonymity of a Pub Choir crowd, people were singing more gently, more thoughtfully. Couch Choir was the sound of humble hopefulness.

ASTRID JORGENSEN

I'll always hold a special place in my memory for all the Couch Choir videos that provided performances I never asked for. We can't fully conceive of anybody but ourselves, so I didn't know of the ways beyond 'singing' that people wanted to contribute to Couch Choir. But I really meant it when I said 'everybody is welcome to join', so I started receiving videos with no singing at all. Videos from people who wanted to contribute by playing their tuba/recorder/kazoo. Choreographed dancing videos from people using movement instead of notes. Videos from non-verbal people in wheelchairs, who nodded their heads silently or banged a drum for three minutes. Then I received a video in American Sign Language.

I watched with awe and wonderment. My worldview had been so narrow, I thought you had to hear music to be part of it. There I was, with three music degrees under my belt, on the global news talking about music accessibility – all the while thinking that music was a collection of sounds. But music is more than noise. Music is a tool to express our humanity to each other in ways that extend beyond words. It hadn't occurred to me to ask the Deaf community to be part of the music. I didn't know any better! But when I received that video in beautiful, fluid sign language, my understanding changed.

Music is just the vehicle: expressing our shared humanity is the destination.

It's a big ask to remember anything I say, but if you take even one message away from this book, let it be this: I think

OLD DOG, NEW TRICKS

you should study sign language. Just consider it. Every culture has its own, unique sign language, because every culture has its own, unique Deaf people. Inspired by Couch Choir and egged on by Waveney, I signed up to study Auslan (Australian sign language) and I kept going until I had my diploma three years later. I'm not fluent and I should definitely practise more, but one of the things I learned is that, just like singing, everybody can learn to sign. But not everybody can learn to hear. It only seems fair to level the playing field a bit.

That one video opened my mind. Music is more than a distraction, or a collection of soundwaves. It really *is* for everybody.

Unless . . . you're autotuning dogs for an online ad campaign and calling it Pup Choir. Then the music isn't that deep and meaningful. In my defence, the company approached *me* first. And it's probably the most I've ever laughed about anything. I would have done anything to keep paying my crew and keep my mind busy – and I did. To me, nothing represents the strangeness of my Covid experience better than that video. I checked YouTube while writing this chapter to see how many views 'Pup Choir' managed to accumulate. The company wanted a huge viral video moment. Five years on, at the time of writing this, it's up to 104 views (sorrrrry).

Thankfully, Pub Choir (for humans) came back into venues. I've since completed whole tours of the USA without a single skid emergency. Now, I have a multi-year visa. Best of all, Gerry comes to enjoy the show as a guest, without having to glue a single poster on a lamppost in New York City.

PIVOT

When December 2021 rolled around, my work situation was so dire that I decided to risk my life by getting twelve metres high, untethered, on a scissor lift.

At this time I, like many others, had been sitting unwashed at home for nearly two years, staring at my computer screen, doomscrolling my phone and descending into madness. (I send eternal gratitude to frontline workers who slogged it out during this time.) I'd stopped wearing pants for online meetings – and also altogether. The novelty of baking sourdough from scratch had long since worn off, and now there were weevils in that 12.5 kilogram sack of flour I'd bought from Aldi.

I probably don't need to go over it – if you have the reading comprehension skills to tackle this book in 2025, you can definitely remember the Covid pandemic all by yourself. The information I will repeat, however, is that at that time in Australia – and in many places around the world – it was specifically illegal to sing in a room with other people.

I understand and support the reasoning (but don't get me started on how the government and media presented live music as inherently more dangerous than sporting events, or politicians hosting private dinner parties). What's undeniable, however, is that the prohibition of 'singing together' was bad for my singing-together business. I did not have the mental fortitude to return to the classroom as a teacher. So, I had to invent something else to do. *Again.*

I had already pivoted (can this word ever feel good again?) in March 2020 by transforming my live Pub Choir show into Couch Choir: a free, online singing experience. But eighteen months in, everybody was sick of singing online. Can you blame them? I couldn't. By that stage, I was screen fatigued – and just generally fatigued – along with everybody else. Which brings me back to my foray into the world of high-visibility workwear and heavy machinery.

It was John who suggested it. He'd received an email from a promotions company, asking if Pub Choir would run a pre-show activity at the premiere of an upcoming kids' movie. Apparently, the distance between cinema seats would satisfy Covid safety restrictions, and this PR team thought a singalong would be a fun, attention-grabbing bit of content to capture. But I couldn't see how being the face of this event would be a good look in the public's eye. Singing together indoors had been specifically demonised as *the* most dangerous, aerosol-spreading activity, which would certainly lead to the downfall of humanity if anybody so much as uttered 'do-re-mi' in a closed space.

That's when John said, 'Why don't we use their idea but take it outside to a drive-in cinema?'

This suggestion felt sparkly to me. Here was a PR company already interested in working together to launch a movie in an unusual way. Surely, we could convince them to relocate the idea outdoors. People could have a sing within their Covid-safe bubbles (their cars) and we wouldn't be breaking any public health rules. If we co-opted the sound system, my instructions could be broadcast via radio frequency to the audience's cars. And if I put my slide deck up on the enormous fifty-metre movie screen, would that be the world's largest-ever PowerPoint presentation? (When is Microsoft gonna sponsor me already, oh my *GOD*?)

'Let's do it!' I cackled to John. 'Imagine everybody honking their car horns instead of cheering.'

We laughed about how happy and strange the idea seemed. 'Everybody is so bored at home,' he said. 'Especially with kids, I reckon everybody will love going as a family!'

'Plus, this will surely be a world first!' I replied.

We were egging each other on. Pub Choir at the drive-in movies, where everybody could hang about afterwards to watch an advanced screening of a new feature film. The only real problem we could see (hello, foreshadowing) was that there wasn't a stage on which to perform.

It is incredibly expensive to get somebody to build a stage. Sometimes I suspect people don't know that running an event has overhead costs. Let's not get into that now, just take my word for it: if you have to build structures for your show, the construction will cost you more than you'll make on tickets (unless you're at a Taylor Swift level). And in this scenario, the audience would be spread out across a huge car lot, and I'm about the same height as Hollywood actor Danny DeVito. I am not visible at the best of times. This show would require some fairly grand staging, and unless I could think of a workaround, the entire gig would be a financial loss – in other words: not a good enough reason for me to put on my pants and leave the house.

'What's that machine you drive around and pull a lever to go up really high?' I asked John. (I don't know anything about construction equipment.)

'A forklift?' he guessed.

'No,' I said. 'It's the thing where somebody stands on a little mechanical platform that goes up and down so they can, I dunno . . . paint stuff and clean windows or something.'

'A cherry picker?'

We looked at pictures of cherry pickers on our phones.

'Hmm, no. It needs to be a machine that's wide enough for two people so Waveney can play her guitar next to me.' I don't know about building equipment, but I watch a lot of movies. I wondered what the machine was that Amy Adams rode to meet the aliens in the movie *Arrival* (to save you googling, it was a scissor lift). 'A scissor lift!' I said, clapping my paws. 'Let's hire a scissor lift as a stage!'

And so we did. John arranged for a two-person scissor lift to be delivered on show day. I could manoeuvre the platform bit of the machine twelve metres in the air with Waveney next to me strumming her guitar – and the ground-based audience would be able to see it all from their cars. If we cable-tied some floodlights to the railing and pointed them towards us, it'd be just like a real stage. *Why aren't more performers cutting their costs by using construction equipment for staging?* I wondered, as I signed a waiver to confirm that I have no regard for my personal safety.

I announced the event online and tickets sold out quickly: 300 cars, filled with potentially 1500 people, were on their way to the drive-in-cinema. It would be most people's first live music experience in nearly two years! My voxmap PowerPoint slides would be projected onto an enormous cinema screen – it always makes me laugh to see my DIY graphics in grand places. And I'd be operating some kind of dangerous machine that would make me seem very practical and tough. I was excited and optimistic about the show, and felt proud to have found a way to keep singing.

To save you the trouble of wondering, let me say definitively that a scissor lift is not a viable stage. Yes, it *is* a lot cheaper than building a stage, but that's because it fucking sucks.

On the day of the show, the scissor lift arrived on the back of a truck and was offloaded onto an *almost* flat bit of gravel. Waveney climbed onto the tiny metal platform and I followed gingerly behind. I say 'gingerly' because, of course,

I was nervous to operate a scissor lift with no experience, but we'd also been instructed to wear fluorescent orange vests. For safety, I think? Probably to safely ensure we would never attempt this madness again. We donned our ginger safety vests and our hard hats, and unlocked our knees in anticipation.

After a four-second induction, a switch was flipped and up we jolted. Waveney steered the scissor lift to its absolute maximum height. Even with the scissory bits fully extended, we were barely visible from the carpark. The platform immediately began to sway. A burp, a fart, a nose scratch or any miniscule movement made it worse. Vigorous guitar-strumming or arm-waving had us rollicking in the open seas: not ideal, given the nature of the show. Also not great: the only way to power the scissor lift, microphones and floodlights was to run an extension cord for 100 metres over the gravelled area through which the cars would be driving and parking. That fact is worth remembering (something I wish I'd said to myself at the time).

Showtime rolled around, and the cars rolled slowly in. It looked like some kind of commotion at the entrance was holding up the line – I could see headlights snaked around the car park and out onto the road where traffic was at a standstill. Whatever the cause, it was just as well because I'd not properly factored in the setting of the sun. Although the show was supposed to be starting, the sun's rays were hitting the screen at just the right/wrong angle to completely obscure my PowerPoint instructions. Nobody could see the words to sing, and nobody could drive into the drive-in. It felt better to wait.

Thirty minutes passed by. The sun was off the screen but loads of cars were still banked up by the entrance for some reason. They were trickling in so slowly. *What's the hold up?* Forty minutes.

The promotion company started getting antsy: if I delayed the show much longer, the feature film would start too late into the evening and the audience wouldn't stay to watch the movie which was supposed to be the reason for the event.

So I decided to start. It's always my call, and I called it. I gave a thumbs up to the distant, earth-bound figure of John, meaning: 'time to get singing'. John flicked some switches then held up two thumbs to me in return. I tested the microphone to make sure it was connected to everybody's car radio:

'Check one, two. Can you hear me from your cars?'

The cars responded, **HONK, HONK, HONK** (I figured honks meant 'yes'.)

'Okay, well I know some of you are still waiting to drive in through the gates, but I've got to get this show on the road . . .' (I paused for laughter before realising I couldn't hear anybody anyway.) 'So . . . feel free to sing along from wherever you are, and hopefully you'll be inside the carpark soon!'

HONK, HONNNNNNK (Maybe those honks meant 'no', but unfortunately I don't speak honk.)

Pub Choir usually works on the principle that I give an instruction, then listen to the audience's response and adjust my next instruction accordingly. But when I can't hear the audience (for instance, if they're sitting inside their cars 100 metres away from me and can only communicate in honks), once I give my instruction, I have to *guess* what people have sung and how I can help them. I have to play the role of both teacher and student and I'm trapped in an unending, imaginary conversation with myself.

'Right. So, I'll sing something first and then you repeat after me.'

I sang the first line of the song and waited for the amount of time needed for the audience to repeat it back.

'So . . . yes. You've, um, probably done a great job of that! Or . . . maybe you didn't? Well done! Or . . . bad job. Haha, okay, uh . . . maybe let's try it again? Just in case. Right. So, I'll sing something first and you repeat after me.'

Repeat ad nauseam.

During this echo-chamber performance, I was also non-consensually feasting upon moths. The floodlights we'd attached to the scissor lift railing were shining only a few centimetres from my face and were attracting *billions* of bugs (a conservative estimate). As Waveney and I swayed back and forth in the air, the swarms of moths were fluttering in and around my every orifice. Whenever I sang, in they came.

There I was, swinging about at twelve metres elevation, eating bugs and delivering my music lesson to honking, parked cars. It was pure mania.

And then the power went out. Of course it did. The lights suddenly cut to black, my wireless microphone disconnected from the radio system, and the scissor lift made those 'powering down' sort of noises. *What the fuck am I doing with my life?* I nihilistically wondered as yet another moth flew up my nose and lodged forever inside my brain. Now the cars were beeping again. I snuck a peek over the edge of the scissor lift (oh, that's right, I'm scared of heights) – which of course sent the whole platform into a new dimension. I yelled out to the tiny figure of Paris below me, 'WHAT . . . THE FUCK . . .' *HONK-HONK* 'IS HAPPENING?'

I saw Paris scurry away to try and find out. *Ughhh vertigo. I should stop looking down*, I thought queasily. I looked across to Waveney, who was clutching her guitar in her high-visibility workwear with her feet spread firmly apart as she surfed through the air, trying desperately to stay alive. I looked up to the moon and embraced my new life as a moth. *I'm ready to go . . .*

Paris interrupted my metamorphosis by shouting something in the distance.

'A LITTLE BOY . . .' *HONK-HONK* 'TRIPPED OVER . . . THE EXTENSION CORD . . . AND KNOCKED OUT ALL THE POWER!' *HONK-HONK* . . . 'WE PLUGGED IT BACK IN AGAIN . . . SO JUST . . . WAIT THERE!'

My sweet summer child, where else would I wait? We are trapped in the air. This is how I die.

'OKAY!' I yelled back.

A minute later, the power returned. The floodlights flickered on and briefly lured the moths away from all my holes. I tested the microphone again. 'One, two. Hello, can you hear me?'

HONK! HONK! HONK!

I made it to the end of the lesson. Heroic, if I do say so myself. Because I couldn't hear anybody singing, I asked people to film themselves singing inside their cars – almost like a hybrid Couch Choir session. They could email those videos to Pub Choir so we (Paris) could compile all the car performances together into one production. Everybody sang what they'd learned and submitted their videos. The show was done. Somebody start the feature film! *Honk-honk!*

Waveney lowered the scissor lift back down and we two moth women tumbled out onto the sweet, sweet ground. I had this sick satisfaction that something unique had just happened. A new human experience unfolded in that place and I had facilitated it. It was definitely weird, and it was hard, but it was also rare and real. I felt brave! Triumphant! Wobbly but good! For ten whole seconds!

I opened my phone and was swarmed with a billion complaints. I can summarise them into three categories:

1. *The traffic was terrible – you should have waited longer before starting. We felt ignored. Very disappointing Pub Choir show.*

2. *You shouldn't have waited so long to start. We sat in terrible traffic for ages and you made us wait even longer. We felt ignored. Very disappointing Pub Choir show.*

3. *This was nowhere near as good as your gigs before Covid. Very disappointing Pub Choir show.*

Look, I'm sure some people had a lovely, or even just a neutral, time at the drive-in that evening. Okay maybe, like, twenty people. But they're never the ones who send an ALL-CAPS email. Enough people were dissatisfied. It was clear I had failed. I let everybody down while I was twelve metres in the air.

One lesson about performing that I've had to learn very publicly, is that at every single show, some people *will* leave disappointed. Even on a good day. And certainly not everybody wants to watch some speck of a woman eating moths and having a psychotic episode at the drive-in. While I'm sure I would enjoy watching that, I understand that not everybody else does. And no matter how well intentioned I am, or how hard I try, people who come to my show will feel what they feel, regardless of what I hoped for. It's a hard-hatted fact of life: if you put yourself out there on a scissor lift, some people will watch your performance/mental breakdown from inside their car and decide that your show sucks.

On this occasion, I think they were probably correct.

It reminds me of that quote somebody said, which I've tried to unsuccessfully locate. Maybe it was Charles Beaumont? I can't find it. Anyway, whoever said it, it's along these poorly paraphrased lines: 'Creativity is like climbing a pile of shit to pick the single rose at the summit, only to realise that along the way you've lost your sense of smell.'

I felt as though I'd been climbing Shit Mountain for eighteen months, unable but desperate to make music with others. This drive-in singalong idea had looked, to me, like a beautiful rose. So I hired a scissor lift and scaled that stinky summit (if only twelve metres high), to find out that it was *not* a beautiful rose growing at the top. It was a swarm of 1 billion moths and 1500 kind-hearted people whom I managed to annoy.

Writing about it now with a few years of emotional distance, I pigheadedly regret nothing. Can you believe *that's* my takeaway?! If you came along to this insane show, thank you for trusting me. I will never take anyone's support for granted. From the bottom of my heart: I'm sorry I let you down. But I also don't regret trying.

I want to be a problem-solver. I'm occasionally willing to put on my pants to go on adventures. I want to experience new things that nobody has ever experienced before – even if it means ruling those things out in the future and being an example to others of 'what not to do'. I want to climb Shit Mountain for the twelve-metre-high views. I want to smell the roses.

GOSSIP GIRL

A social media post by Hugh Jorgensen dated 18 November 2014:

My sister Astrid is currently performing on stage with the Rolling Stones. Any pretence that Timothy, Malcolm, Phillip and I were in a fair contest for our parents' love is now over.

At least half of that post is true. At that moment, I was onstage with the Rolling Stones. The actual band. Like, *the* Rolling Stones. They were onstage performing their music, and I was also on that same stage at the same time. I'm not sure if you're getting it? I – Astrid Jorgensen – conducted for one of the most famous bands of all time.

It sounds more impressive than it actually was, but that would never stop me from milking the anecdote. I guess I could reluctantly admit that no member of the Rolling

Stones has any idea who I am and wouldn't recognise me in a police lineup. But in 2014, the band's management contacted my music mentor Dr James Cuskelly, and asked him if he knew of a high-quality, Brisbane-based choir with twenty-four members, who might like to sing for the Rolling Stones. James, the living legend, said 'yes' and made up a choir on the spot. He called it Vibrancy.

Working backwards from securing the gig of a lifetime, James sent around an email to twenty-four colleagues and ex-students, of which I was one. In his email to me, he tried to be coy.

> *James:* I have the chance for a small group (24) to be a backing choir for a rather famous touring rock group in November – interested in being part of that?? Need to just sort out who we will include!

> *Me:* I just so happen to know that the Rolling Stones will be here in November. Don't respond to this speculation, I need to see the whites of your eyes before I take you seriously.

He was serious. Of course, I immediately screeched 'yes', as did twenty-three other singers. The Rolling Stones's management then emailed James again to say that the choir would need to be split half-and-half across the stage. As such, he would be conducting on one side of the stage, but had to nominate another member of Vibrancy to conduct the opposite side. And James chose me.

I stood in front of my half of Vibrancy (the made-up choir) with 10,000 people cheering behind me, and waved my arms while the Rolling Stones performed 'You Can't Always Get What You Want'. Annoyingly, I can't remember much of what happened onstage because I was so nervous that my heartbeat inside my ears was louder than the music and the crowd. But I *can* remember the soundcheck, and thus am extremely happy to bring you the following inside information:

- Mick Jagger wore a kimono to soundcheck. What a comfortable king.
- Mick Jagger did not soundcheck his vocals (not in front of Vibrancy, anyway) but seemed to have a voice double, who checked his microphones for him while he quietly watched on. This has become my benchmark for 'making it' – I'll know I have arrived as a performer when I have a voice doppelganger, who endures my soundchecks for me while I watch on, wearing my kimono.
- I'm quite sure I saw Mick Jagger and Keith Richards warm up their vocals by smoking cigarettes backstage (and also between songs during the concert). I'm not cool enough to be a smoker and I have asthma, but is it wrong to admit that I think cigarettes look incredibly cool because of this core memory: seeing Mick and Keith hoof durries backstage at the show?

I assumed then that sharing a stage with the Rolling Stones would be my one and only celebrity encounter in life.

I've since had the privilege of interacting with loads of extraordinarily talented artists. In doing so, I've learned many interesting things about certain famous people. And I would love to tell you these stories because I think you would find them fascinating, but I also don't want to be a snitch.

As a compromise, I've decided to write two lists. On one list, you'll find the names of some of the remarkable celebrities with whom my path has crossed. The other list shows my summary of our interaction. **Very important to note: the two lists do not line up.** Your job is to draw a line between who you believe matches each one-line summary. I will never reveal the answers and there is no prize.

The Celebrity	Astrid's Summary
Sir Barry Gibb (from The Bee Gees)	Has *really* nice cushions at their house
Kate Bush (singer/songwriter)	Very good at doing 'the worm' as a dance move
Radiohead (the band)	The most nervous (extremely endearing)
Neil Finn (from Crowded House)	I accidentally called them to ask if we need bread while I was grocery shopping (thought I was dialling Evyn)
Mark Seymour (from Hunters & Collectors)	The most drunk (not endearing)
Felix Riebl (from The Cat Empire)	The most drug-affected (not endearing at all)

The Celebrity	Astrid's Summary
Judith Lucy (Australian comedian)	The most shy (extremely endearing)
Ella Hooper (from Killing Heidi)	The outright winner. Kind, supportive, hilarious and clever
Ben Lee (singer/songwriter)	Changed my life forever – thank you
Karl Stefanovic (Australian TV presenter)	Needed help finding the first beat of their own song
John Collins (from Powderfinger)	Really, really cared that the performance was good
Tim Freedman (from The Whitlams)	Reached out, but I accidentally ignored them and missed my chance to connect
Sticky Fingers (the band)	The most horrible to work with by such a large margin – *everybody* tried to warn me
Paul Kelly (singer/songwriter)	Beloved by straight women and rightfully so
Samuel Johnson (Australian actor)	I immediately understood their appeal when up close
Rachel Griffiths (Australian actress)	Straight women BEWARE
Dave Faulkner (from Hoodoo Gurus)	Suggested that I should be sent to North Korea
Ben Ely (from Regurgitator)	Called to ask if they should start drinking hard liquor to achieve a lower-sounding voice

The Celebrity	Astrid's Summary
Brendan B. Brown (from Wheatus)	Their private persona is the exact opposite of how they portray themselves in public (not a compliment)
Meg Mac (singer/songwriter)	Understandably weirded out by how much I proclaimed my love and had to ask me to leave their dressing room
Dr Karl Kruszelnicki (Australian science presenter and author)	Cares the most about what people think of them (rich coming from me!)
Julia Zemiro (Australian actress and TV presenter)	Made me believe you can be a professional artist and a kind, balanced person
Kevin Rudd (former prime minister of Australia)	So humble, so chatty, so genuinely interested. Wish we were besties
Anthony Albanese (current Prime Minister of Australia)	Truly hated Pub Choir. Sent their invoice *during* the show and had left before I'd walked off stage

If you are one of those listed, feel free to assume that my best summary is referring to you. Let's work together soon, okay? Except if you're . . . *them*.

THE ELEPHANT IN THE ROOM

I recently saw one of my heroes, the author Fran Lebowitz, give a talk in Brisbane. After she had finished, the audience was invited to call out questions for Fran to answer. Somebody near me stood up and yelled out: 'What's your favourite book?' I paraphrase her response:

'I wish people would stop asking me what my favourite "something" is,' Fran said in her iconic, fast-paced, New York accent. 'It's such a childish question. What's your favourite *colour*, what's your favourite *ice cream* flavour?' she mocked. (Could I love her any more?) 'Do you see how old I am? Favourites are something that children have. You ask a child what their favourite ice-cream flavour is, and they say "vanilla" because they've only tasted three flavours of ice cream. I'm not five years old! I've tasted too much ice cream to have a favourite. I've read too many books. I know too much. No more questions about favourites.'

A roar of approval went up around the concert hall. We all cheered at this iconically 'Fran' answer. Then the next three people proceeded to ask Fran what her favourite movie, painting and city other than New York was. I nearly cringed to death.

I've since banked a variation of Fran's answer in case of emergency. Given I'm not a seventy-four-year-old feminist literary icon, I tone it down a bit. But if you ask me what my favourite song is, I don't know. I've heard too many songs. No single song is the right song all the time. If I want to listen to music, I go into my pharmacy of songs and select the one I need for my ailment. Feeling a bit low? Maybe I'll listen to something wordless and melancholy, so I can really wallow in my self-pity. Feeling tired? An upbeat 1990s R&B number will snap me out of it. Feeling the most ashamed I've ever felt? The song doesn't matter, I just need something to yell myself hoarse. The right tune is always changing, depending on what medicine I need.

If you ask me what my favourite Pub Choir show is, my answer would be similarly obtuse. I don't know, because it depends on what synonym you'd use to replace the word 'favourite'. The musical arrangement I'm the most *proud* of? My version of Paul Kelly's 'How To Make Gravy', performed in Brisbane, 2018. Most emotionally moved I've ever felt at a show? The final night I taught Toto's 'Africa' in Melbourne, 2023. Most enthusiastic audience response? The Dream Academy's 'Life in a Northern Town' in Brisbane, 2019. As you can see, that question has many answers.

If you ask me about my *least* favourite Pub Choir show, however, I know the answer. There have been a few absolute flops, for sure, but no matter how you look at it, I immediately know which one was the worst.

I don't want the people in this story being further tormented, so I've changed some identifying details. But the real memory of this show haunts me as I close my eyes to sleep. I will never forget it. Any time I think a show is tough, or not going as well as I'd hoped, I remember *the* show. And then I think, *Well, at least it's not as bad as that.*

I suppose it's taught me gratitude (in the worst possible way), which is a reason to tell this story. I think it's important to always have some perspective. When you're a performer and you bomb at a show, it helps you appreciate the shows where you don't bomb. Even dead-average shows seem fine when you remember how disgraced you were that one time. It helps you to develop a horrid, necessary gratefulness through public humiliation. It all counts for something, right? That's what I tell myself.

This worst show also changed Pub Choir's current show for the better, so that's important.

Look at me delaying telling you the story! You'll see why. In this story, I behaved like a selfish monster. I know we all do that sometimes, but the odds are, I probably won't hear about the time *you* were a selfish monster, but you will read about mine in great detail. So I guess I'll go first and hope you can remember that it's my first time being alive and I'm trying my best.

Really, the main reason I'm going to share this awful story is to apologise again to the person in a wheelchair who was trying to get away from me, who I chased down a road late at night, flanked by thirty drunk people and four men disguised as elephants.

So . . . here I go.

,

My crew and I have arrived onsite early to scope out the venue. The manager comes out to greet us unsmilingly and walks us through the downstairs area, which is essentially a pokies (slot-machine) arcade. We stroll through the patterned carpet corridors of machines as they flash their lights and spew their robotic music. Slumped in front of the machines are transfixed oldies, clutching huge cups filled with their children's inheritance.

The manager leads us to a staircase and points to the top. 'Do the show up there. Should have everything youse need.' And off he fucks. We climb the stairs and find a concreted room filled with conference chairs. There's no stage, no sound system and nobody to help.

'We'll have to grab our own sound system from the van and carry all the gear up these stairs,' John says.

'Can't the venue manager give us a hand?' I ask, knowing that he absolutely won't give us a hand.

We do what we can to make this space viable for the show. Without a stage, I pick a corner of the room. Paris and

THE ELEPHANT IN THE ROOM

John set up a projector screen, and place some speakers on the floor. Jacob (photographer) moves all the chairs to one side and clears the space. It will have to do. There is no greenroom or backstage area, so once we've decided everything is in place, Waveney and I just stand in the corner, waiting for the audience to arrive.

Some locals start trickling in and head straight for the makeshift bar (an esky and some crates of hard liquor) at the back of the room. It gets rowdy very quickly. Every voice bounces off the concrete floor and accumulates. The rise in volume is matched only by the spike in everybody's blood-alcohol level. This is going to be a rough show.

Five long minutes to go. Three more excruciating minutes. One infinite minute.

At the very last second, a member of the bar staff comes to shout in my ear. 'There's a man downstairs who can't get inside.'

'What do you mean, he can't get inside. Is he too drunk?' I ask.

'Nah, he literally can't get in. He's in a wheelchair. His wife seems pretty pissed off and asked to speak to you.'

A hot worry surges through my body like a lightning strike. I scurry through the audience and run downstairs, three at a time. At the bottom of the stairs are a man and woman in their thirties. They're both wearing matching button-up, plaid flannel shirts and long tan-coloured trousers with brown leather work boots. He is sitting in a wheelchair and she is standing behind him.

The woman looks angry. 'We can't get up the stairs and there's no lift. This is bullshit!' she says.

'Oh my *GOD*, I'm so sorry. There will be a way around the back or something. Let me find the venue manager. I'll get you in, I promise,' I falsely promise, turning and preparing to run for help.

'We already spoke with him and there's no way in,' she calls out.

My heart sinks. I turn back towards her.

'He said something about the building being heritage listed so they aren't required to be accessible. Which would have been *great* for you to tell people when they went to book tickets.'

'Oh noooo. I'm so sorry,' I say.

'Yeah, well, "sorry" won't get us up the stairs. We drove for hours to get here. And now we can't even go in. Seriously, this is disgraceful. Shame on you.'

I immediately feel the shame upon me.

I look at man in the wheelchair. The right side of his face is drooped. His left hand is clutched tightly by his side. Guilt wraps its fingers around my throat, but I try to ignore this feeling and think of a solution.

'I have a crew with me. There are some strong men upstairs, can we carry you in your chair? They will be so happy to help! We'll do anything to make it work, I'm really sorry!' I bleat.

The man says nothing and lowers his eyes to his lap. I look hopefully to the woman but she steps forward around

THE ELEPHANT IN THE ROOM

the wheelchair. The anger in her eyes has already turned to sadness.

In a low voice, she says, 'The wheelchair is a very recent development in our lives. We're not comfortable making a scene. I know he wouldn't want people handling him or his chair. He just wanted to get inside like everybody else.'

I am nodding emphatically, as if I know exactly where they're coming from (I don't know).

She sighs, 'I guess we'll just sit downstairs and listen. What else can we do? We travelled here just for your show.' She looks defeated. I did this. Guilt grips my neck.

I can hear a slurred chant starting upstairs from the 250 people who are waiting for the show to start. 'Pub Choir! Pub Choir! Pub Choir!' A few jeers and whistles are being thrown in. I'm late for my worst-ever show.

I look at the man and woman in turn. Every word trips out of my mouth at an unusually high pitch and speed. 'I'm so sorry. It's unforgivable. Obviously, we'll get your tickets refunded. And it's my fault for not checking about the stairs. I would never have booked this venue if I knew. I'm so ashamed that this is happening. I . . . I don't know how to fix this.' Tears are gathering in the corners of my eyes.

The woman shrugs. 'You can't fix this, it's too late now.'

So not knowing what else to do, I turn my back on them and run back up the stairs, dabbing my eyes.

I arrive back in the gig area. It's unbelievably loud. I try to gather my thoughts. Pub Choir's motto is 'singing belongs to everyone', but it turns out that it *doesn't* belong to everybody if you're careless about accessibility. Downstairs are two people who paid with their money and time to *not* have access to my show. I can give them back their money. I can't give them back their time.

I look around me at all the people who are already sloppily drunk. I elbow my way through them to the non-existent stage in the corner. Somebody in the audience spots me pushing my way through the crowd and points. A cheer goes up in the room, but not the kind that ends quietly. The noise in the room grows exponentially. I want the floor to crack open and swallow me into the earth.

I yell into the microphone, 'Welcome to Pub Choir!'

Two or three people up the front clap then give up. Nobody else responds. Some kind of possession takes hold of me and I remove the microphone from the stand to start roving throughout the room. I try to get the audience's attention by getting close and getting loud.

'WELCOME TO THE SHOW. WE'RE GOING TO LEARN A SONG. LET'S GET SINGING.'

The sound of people ignoring me.

I walk right up to people's faces and address them personally, trying to get their attention. 'ARE YOU READY TO SING, SIR?' I am fifteen centimetres from a man's face, yelling.

'Waheyyyyyy,' he drunkenly replies.

This is a nightmare. I feel like I'm yelling into an industrial fan. I get angry.

'The show has STARTED but some of you have obviously

just come here to talk. So if you want to talk, please FUCK OFF downstairs coz we're about to sing in this room.'

Immediate, terrible silence. Now everybody is offside. Fantastic.

'Get on with it,' somebody calls out. A few people laugh in agreement.

'I am TRYING TO if you would all stop rudely talking and listen to me,' I snap back.

A couple of boos from the back of the room.

'This show *sucks*,' says somebody else. They're not wrong. This show does suck. People are leaving before it's even begun.

I try not to spiral. I look over at Waveney with pleading eyes to start the show. Waveney co-wrote a beautiful Acknowledgement of Country song to pay respects to the Traditional Owners of the land, and every Pub Choir show has been starting in this way. She launches into her song, and we sing it as a duet, but the crowd chatter immediately starts up again. This time less chirpy. More people peel away from the back of the room and head downstairs. It's an exodus.

I begin my choir lesson but I've lost my sense of humour and I can't sense it anywhere. The only way is through, so I forge on. More people leave. I go through the motions, I do not cry. I try to find my way back to sounding enthusiastic. I sing through my arrangement line by line and click through my slides and I seem to win a few people back. Maybe thirty *very* kind people stay to learn the song to completion. It sounds a mess, but I think I've done enough to end the show.

'Let's sing this song one final time and call it a night,' I announce to the stayers. Then I spot the woman from downstairs. She's standing alone up the back of the room. She must have popped in to see a few minutes of my show. My unbearable, inaccessible show.

An idea strikes me. *What if, as a group, we all walk downstairs and sing for the man in the wheelchair?*

'Give me ONE second!' I tell the audience as I rush over to the woman to communicate my idea. She says she'll go downstairs and ask if her husband would like us to bring our performance to him.

I don't wait for approval. My panic has made me thoughtless and arrogant. I let my saviour complex take the wheel and I decide that approval is *definitely* on the way.

So I make an announcement to the audience: 'Everyone! A slight change of plan! I need your help. My motto at Pub Choir is that "singing belongs to everyone", but there's somebody downstairs in a wheelchair who couldn't come to this show because of the stairs.'

Why am I betraying his privacy to this group of unruly strangers?

The audience let's out a big, pitying 'awwww'. I have their full attention for the first time tonight. 'So I was wondering if you'd all come down the stairs with me and sing what we've learned for him?'

Why am I inserting myself into somebody else's sadness?

The audience cheers. They turn and chatter excitedly to each other about this side quest.

THE ELEPHANT IN THE ROOM

'Okay!' I say, capitalising on this newfound focus. 'Grab everything from this room and let's head downstairs to sing for our mate!' More whoops from the audience.

I hurry ahead of the pack, so I can go and tell the man and the woman my good news: that I have solved everything, and that I am a hero.

They are nowhere to be seen.

I frantically flit about the pokies room, searching.

The audience is now descending the stairs, led by four men carrying huge, cardboard cut outs. I hadn't noticed until this moment, but inaccessibility was not the only elephant in the room. By the door, for reasons unknown to me, was a herd of gigantic cardboard elephants. When I said 'Grab everything from this room,' these blokes picked up four of the enormous figurines and are now using them as performance props.

I spin back around in one last desperate attempt to find the man and woman. I spot them. Maybe forty metres away, heading off quietly into the dark is the silhouette of a wife pushing her husband's wheelchair. In this moment, I could have let them disappear into the night. But I chose fuckwittery. I *chased* them. The elephant cut-out men saw me running, assumed it was a game and followed clumsily behind me.

I am now chasing the man and the woman down the road. And a herd of elephants is chasing all of us.

I arrive at the married couple first. Thankfully, the elephants keep a respectful distance. I pathetically call out,

'Don't leave yet! We've all come to sing for you!' The woman turns towards me with a crushed expression. She speaks.

'We were going to stay, but then we realised there wasn't even an accessible toilet downstairs. My husband really needed to use the toilet and there wasn't one and . . . now it's too late. Please just let us go. *Please*. Don't let those people see us like this.'

I made *them* beg *me* for mercy.

The woman turns away and pushes her husband's wheelchair into the shadows of the night. Behind me, four elephants are doing the can-can. Behind them, thirty people are cheering by the light of the pokies. I turn to face the music. I want to howl and rip off my skin. I wish a herd of wild elephants would trample me to dust. Instead, I gather the cardboard cut-out crew and rejoin the crowd.

'They had to go!' I say in a high-pitched squeak, hoping I sound cheerful and unbothered. The mob lets out a second pitying 'Awwww.'

'Well, let's just sing the song anyway and then you can all go home,' I suggest, needing this to be over.

Nobody knows the words because my instructional slides are still being projected onto the wall upstairs. But I know the words. So I kick off my shoes and climb barefoot onto the closest chair and tell Waveney to play her guitar. There are no speakers for her guitar, no microphone for my voice. Analogue, I sing the song at the top of my lungs, indicating to the crowd they should sing anything they can remember. We all shriek horribly for three minutes. Feeling the most ashamed I've ever felt, the song doesn't matter anymore. I just need something to yell myself hoarse.

The audience offers a smattering of applause at the end of this 'performance', then immediately disperses into the glow of the pokies. I climb down from the chair and walk barefoot, alone, into the surrounding darkness.

I cup both my guilty hands around my neck and I cry, and cry, and cry.

These days, I check that my venues are wheelchair accessible. With the urgency of being chased by a herd of elephants, I check. I'm really sorry. I'm not even asking for forgiveness. I'm promising to remember. An elephant never forgets.

DON'T SHIT IN GLASS HOUSES

Live music venues having icky greenrooms are a certainty of life. No matter the location or scale of the event, the backstage area will be sticky, dingy and musty, with an endless covering of band signatures and dick drawings on the walls. And there's always a couch stained with a minimum of three types of bodily fluids.

I like the feral nature of these spaces. It makes me feel like cool people have partied hard in this place. I think with pride about that history – certainly not because I consider myself a similarly cool party person, but because I'm sure I am the exact opposite. I'm proud to be invited to the cool kids' room, knowing that I didn't get there through cocaine-fuelled benders, but with PowerPoint presentations.

Surely, my crew and I are the most harmless nerds to ever enter a greenroom. I once glimpsed the backstage rider of an international touring band, who had a few big hits in the 1990s. They had what seemed like an encyclopaedic list of must-have items, including very specific cuts of sandwich meat, a certain brand of condoms and a bottle of Nivea 3-in-1. Shampoo, conditioner and body wash all in one liquid? *Dream on, fellas.*

My Pub Choir rider consists of fresh vegetables, hummus, bags of chips, a few beers and sugar-free soft drinks. In lieu of noisy afterparties with (non-existent) groupies, once my show is over we chat about video games we're playing, or indie movies we've seen lately. Sometimes, nobody says anything and we sit in happy silence, scrolling our phones.

The wildest our greenroom gets is when we play games to pass the time before a show starts. Prepare to be wowed as I count down Pub Choir's five most commonly played backstage games:

5. Paris Fashion Week

Paris Owen, my brilliant videographer, wears the clothes she has in her suitcase. All at the same time, Michelin-man style. As a group, we call out what we think the next layer will be:

'Horizontal navy-and-white striped shirt has GOT to be under there!'

'Nah, I think it'll be mustard baseball shirt next, for SURE!'

Once we've made our guesses, she slowly peels off the outermost layer of clothing while we chant maniacally: 'FASHION PARADE! FASHION PARADE!'

We only ever played this game in front of an outsider once. International music legend and pop culture icon

Ben Lee watched us play Paris Fashion Week backstage. We learned a lot about ourselves and our misconceptions of our social acceptability through his facial expressions. Thank you, Ben. We needed to know.

4. What time is it?

This is self-explanatory. Nobody is allowed to look at their phones or a clock, and we guess the time based on feel. This is actually quite fun when we're unbelievably jet-lagged and have lost all sense of time and place. Paris Owen, of Paris Fashion Week, is great at this game. We refer to her as the Time Lord.

3. How long's it been?

Somebody is appointed Time Keeper, and at a random moment of their choosing, they announce the game has started. They alone know the time at that moment. We resume our conversations or our show preparation and generally go about our lives. Later, again without warning, the Time Keeper will shout: 'How long's it been?' The closest answer wins. Everybody is bad at this one.

2. Spot the difference

This game is occasionally aired in front of outsiders. We nominate a backstage contestant to stare at a certain section of the greenroom to memorise as much of the scene as possible. Then, they leave the room and we rearrange the space in subtle ways. Somebody might turn a beer can 180 degrees so the label faces the other way. A single fork may be hidden. Occasionally, two people will swap shirts. It's terribly difficult. The contestant re-enters and we yell: 'Spot! The! Difference!' With no visual memory, I am undeniably the worst at this game.

1. Where's Astrid's clicker?

We play this one the most by far, but I guess it's less of a game and more of a team-building activity. As in, nobody participates by choice, and their boss (me) forces them to play.

Pub Choir's live show relies heavily on my PowerPoint presentations, which I control using a thin, silvery clicker device. It's about the width of a cigarette lighter and the length of a small Asian woman's hand. How perfect. I am at one with my clicker. My clicker feels such a natural part of me, it often doesn't occur to me that I'm still holding it in the greenroom, at the merch desk or in the bathroom. Nine times out of ten, as I get dressed for the show, eat my dinner or reach for the toilet paper, I absent-mindedly leave my clicker somewhere without noticing it was ever there, or that it is now gone.

Once I finally realise it's lost, I slink back to the group and shyly ask, 'Where's Astrid's clicker?'

Everyone sighs and stands up to look. Thankfully, we always find it.

'It's here in the fridge!'

'It was on the hand dryer in the toilet!'

'I found it in your shoe!'

Oh, how I wish it was just the clicker.

I lose, spill, break, crease and crack everything I own and love. It would genuinely save me time if, at the beginning of every meal, I simply picked up my food and poured it down my front. Instead, I eat slowly, pretending to myself that this will be the meal where I don't stain my clothes. No word of a lie, while drafting this chapter, I read that previous sentence to Evyn over dinner and accidentally knocked an entire plate of hot dumplings onto his lap at the same time.

In our house, my every possession and clothing item is displayed like a grubby floor buffet to be surveyed, picked at and tripped over constantly. I come home from tour and leave my suitcase open, knowing that I'll need all those items again in two weeks, so why bother putting them away at all? Make the bed when I'm just going to mess it up at night? Absolutely not. And I would quite happily live in such filth if it wasn't a constant source of stress for Evyn.

Evyn is a clean person. He showers incessantly, puts all his possessions away and never loses his wallet, keys, phone or laptop – all things that I lose daily. To his great credit, he doesn't seem to be terribly annoyed or upset, and certainly never *surprised*, when I lose my things. Helping me find my possessions has become part of our division of household labour. I am head of procurement, food and adventure. I cook, take care of the groceries and introduce chaos into our lives. In return, Evyn does the bulk of things that require organisation, like paying bills on time, having a day job, tidying the house and finding my things. But given that I often work from home and like to cook multiple splattery meals a day, keeping me tidy is more than a one-person job.

As a peace offering, I hired a professional cleaner, who comes once a fortnight to do things like wipe the benches, put things away and scrub the toilet – all exceedingly achievable tasks for everyone but me. A cleaner was my way of acknowledging that I know I'm a little rat who leaves her mess everywhere, but that I'm also too important to remedy this myself.

It pains me to need a cleaner so badly. But I need a cleaner so badly.

I searched online and found somebody close by. And from my very first interaction with my cleaner, I felt embarrassed about *everything*. They asked if a fortnightly 8 am time slot was okay and, rather than admit that this is my only hour of good sleep, I screamed 'YES!' down the phone with a grotesque amount of enthusiasm. 'Yes, of *course*, 8 am is *great* for me. I would have been up for hours anyway working, because that's why I need a cleaner! I work such long hours, I'm just so busy, that's why all my dirty undies are lying in the exact position where I took them off nine days ago, each leg hole perfectly preserved. I'm actually so clean, I'm just *busy*.'

Lies.

We keep a spare key in a lockbox by the front door for days when Evyn is at work and I'm on tour. But on those occasions when I'm home on a cleaning morning, I set my alarm for 7.58 am. I spring out of bed, don any available clothes from the floor buffet and grab my laptop. I don't brush my teeth, drink water or go to the toilet – THERE IS NO TIME. Because at 7.59 am, the cleaner knocks at our door. I'm already standing directly behind the door, waiting for three seconds so it doesn't seem like I was standing directly behind the door, waiting for them to arrive. I eventually fling the door open and shout with my rancid morning breath, 'Welcome! I'm just heading to the office to do some work, I'll leave you to it.'

I then sneak away into our garden where we have a small shed, which I converted into an office space during Covid lockdowns. It's essentially a glasshouse with a desk and piano in our backyard. When the blinds are raised, you can easily observe from the house what's going on in the shed. I leave the blinds up so the cleaner can see that I'm working while they are working, because we're the same, aren't we? I'm staring blankly at my haggard reflection on my empty laptop screen for two hours, while they scrub encrusted shit off my toilet.

And don't I deserve this for all my hard work?

I sit there for the full two-hour clean. Usually with a throbbing caffeine-withdrawal headache and absolutely busting for the loo. At 10.01 am, I can finally return to the house, go to the toilet and get back into bed. You really go through it when you have a cleaner.

It feels important at this moment to tell you that I live next door to – and downhill from – a home childcare centre. Every day from about 8 am to 4 pm, small children play and cry outside while overlooking my garden with an extremely clear view of everything that happens there. It also feels important to tell you that I'm sorry and to ask that you kindly stop reading this.

,

One fateful morning I opened the door at 7.59 am for my cleaner and performed my usual, ridiculous one-woman, off-Broadway show, Heading to Work. I traipsed down to the shed and slid the glass door closed behind me. I sat at the desk and opened my laptop. And then I felt a truly thunderous pressure in my bowels.

Maybe you can still get a refund on the purchase of this book?

It was immediately clear to me that this was not a fart. It felt very hot and very wrong.

What time is it?

I looked at my watch: 8.03 am. My cleaner always starts with the toilet. At this very moment, they were neck-deep in porcelain. I couldn't imagine a universe where I walked back up to the house, stood behind them, cleared my throat and said, 'Would you mind stepping aside as I freshly crucify this surface that you cleaned not twenty seconds ago? It will definitely need recleaning immediately afterwards. And then you'll need to breathe the stench of whatever demon is trying to get out of me as it engulfs the house for the next fifteen minutes. Is that cool with you?'

I couldn't bring myself to do this. I simply could not. So I clenched with all my might and hoped that whatever this ungodly presence was, it could be reabsorbed into my bloodstream over the next two hours. Surely, my guts didn't extract EVERY nutrient. Have another look, please! *Please?*

I got up and paced about the room to distract myself. *Maybe I should do some actual work. Fire off some emails?* I turned on my laptop and sent off a few terse replies to John about an upcoming tour. *I hope my cleaner is watching.*

How long's it been?

'Okay, it's 8.20 am. I can hold this in for another, what . . . a hundred minutes?'

I have endured bouts of gastro backstage and managed to keep it all in for a full two-hour Pub Choir performance. I've contracted the flu and turned up onstage fatigued, confused, drenched in sweat, shaking. I still finished the show. I've lost my voice in front of 3000 people, and *still* managed to power through and teach them how to sing despite being voiceless myself. Since Pub Choir began, I've been the master of my body and all its holes in many challenging situations. Until this moment.

By 8.25 am, I was sweating profusely. I felt so sick in my down-belows. I sat down to think about my options and suddenly realised that I could not get up again. Whatever intestinal process had been holding back the devil was now at an end. I knew then that all that was between me and spectacularly shitting myself at age thirty-three was the weight of my own body on the chair, plus one atom of epidermis.

Sitting in my glasshouse, a desperate beast, I saw in the distance my cleaner methodically working their way through my kitchen. And my cleaner could see me. I was no longer pretending to work, but just sitting perfectly still. Wide-eyed and glistening. Next door, a toddler began to cry.

Kid, you have no idea.

I rolled my office chair along the floor without daring to break contact with the seat, and started searching for a vessel. A bowl, a box, a bag, *anything*. Over there was an empty fruit basket with thousands of holes. In the other direction, a wastepaper bin with delicate latticed sides and not one centimetre of solid support. I started to properly panic. There was no longer a chance to make it to the house. I wasn't even sure if I could make it ten steps to the grass in the garden and, for God's sake, THE CHILDREN WOULD SEE. (Can you get arrested for indecently defecating in your own yard?)

Oh God, oh God, oh God, oh God.

I looked back at the latticed bin and saw a flash of something reflective. I wheeled myself over. At the bottom of the bin lay a singular, empty chip packet. It's too cruel to describe it as fun-sized. But there it was. The only solid receptacle in that godforsaken place.

At 8.27 am I accepted my fate. I could not make it to ten o'clock. I would not make it out of the room. I was done for.

A reminder that this is all 'opt-in' reading. You can opt out at any time.

I held the miniscule packet in my hands and tried to anticipate the detonation sequence. I guessed I had the time it would take for me to stand up – maybe one second – before the kraken was released from my crack. This would require quick movements and pinpoint arsehole accuracy.

Paris Fashion Week

At 8:30 am I somehow needed to fashion parade my pants off at the exact same time as I stood up, while positioning the un-fun-sized chip packet perfectly. I wheeled to the door and drew down the blinds on all sides.

Forgive me.

What followed was the worst and best thing I've ever done. I did not miss. I stood, I de-panted, I caught the load. It towered high above the chip packet in a truly unexpected solid form. And I caught it. I had it all. I couldn't believe it.

But then I realised that I was standing pant-less in a glasshouse, holding in both hands a warm bag of my own substantial excrement. With ninety minutes to go. Not knowing what else to do, I stood there. I just fucking stood there with my pants around my ankles, looking at what

I had done, for one and a half hours. I felt the warmth slowly drain away, along with any shred of joy or self-respect I had.

At 10.01 am, I carefully pulled up my pants and crab-walked to the house, holding my hazardous waste while praying it was nap time next door. I double, triple, quadruple-bagged my haul. I threw out my pants. I showered and scrubbed until I saw bone.

,

That evening, I admitted everything to Evyn. The horror on his face. The terror in his eyes. Both similar to expressions I'd made earlier in the day, but his driven by the realisation of the kind of person with whom he had co-signed a thirty-year mortgage.

'WHY DIDN'T YOU JUST GO BACK TO THE HOUSE?' he laugh-pleaded. 'WE HAVE TOILETS. THEY WOULD HAVE UNDERSTOOD.'

Of course, I would go back in time if I could. To the time before Evyn found out his girlfriend shat into her own hands and stood there for ninety minutes.

'I don't know, I don't knoooooow,' I moaned. 'I panicked. I waited too long then I couldn't move. Do you still love me? Can you ever love me again?'

He never got time to answer, because at that exact moment, my phone dinged. It dung.

It was a notification from the national news broadcaster, announcing I had been awarded a Medal of the Order of Australia for services to the community as a musical director. Mid-shitting-into-a-bag-confession, I turned the screen to show Evyn the full news story, which was already becoming difficult to read, because text messages and emails had started flooding in.

> *Congratulations Astrid!! I just saw the news!!! You are such an inspiration to us all. Whatever you're doing, keep it up!*

> *Well done Astrid, is there nothing you can't do?!! We are all so proud of what you!! Never change!!!*

> *The nation is cheering for you Astrid, you really deserve this, I hope you're celebrating with Evyn tonight!! Do something really special!*

Each year, about 70,000 people clamour for a ticket to Pub Choir. People clap and cheer for me when I walk onstage. I bounce around full of confidence, zest, encouragement and clarity. I am an extrovert, a leader, a medal winner.

That version onstage is a true part of me. I'm not faking it; those qualities do exist within me. In small amounts. But there is another part of me – a much bigger part. Wrapped in four garbage bags in a waste facility somewhere. Both versions of me are hot shit.

Spot! The! Difference!

JUNE

'Astrid, will you tell me a love story?'

A live audience of 1500 book-lovers sat expectantly as acclaimed and beloved author Trent Dalton asked me this question onstage. My heart was thumping as I prepared to read out a family secret that had never been shared before, and that I'd only heard in full a few days earlier.

This was in September 2021 at Trent's book launch event for his soon-to-be-bestseller, *Love Stories*. Surely one of the most friendly and enthusiastic men alive, Trent had sat behind his typewriter in Brisbane's city centre, asking strangers passing by to tell him a love story. He then compiled these everyday tales of love into a tender collection, with his own stories weaved throughout.

For the book launch, Trent planned to re-enact his *Love Stories* interview process in front of a crowd at City Hall. He asked me to join him onstage where he'd pose to me his catchphrase question. I was invited to respond by reading a prepared paragraph or two for the audience. I thought about the love stories I had to tell and felt inadequate.

Much like being asked how Pub Choir started, my love story with Evyn is quiet and undramatic. To me, our love is a slowly unfolding miracle, enriching every day of my life . . . But that doesn't really function as a snappy crowd-pleasing anecdote. And we all know that the goal of creativity is to quickly impress strangers and loudly compete with other creatives.

Was my love story good enough to tell? I reflected on how Evyn and I met.

In 2025, I will have loved Evyn for more of my life than not. We met at the end of our first year of university, when I was seventeen and he was eighteen. At that time, Evyn wanted to be a writer and I wanted to be a doctor, so in a way we have achieved our goals as a couple.

Back in 2007, we were both fresh out of school and following the ideal study pathway for any high-achieving child: a Bachelor of Arts. Evyn came to my attention because I saw him EVERYWHERE. Why was this red-headed, sharp-nosed, square-jawed boy in every one of my classes, even though I had picked a bizarre and useless mix of subjects? I'd turn up to my ear-training music class, and there he'd be. Then off to my evolutionary psychology lecture, where he was already seated in the front row. Think I could learn about mitochondria, the powerhouse of the cell, without distraction? Not a chance with Evyn sitting behind me in

JUNE

Introductory Biology. Statistics 101? Modern Composing Techniques? You've got to be kidding me! *What a stalker.*

Like all great love stories throughout the ages, we don't remember who made the first move. At some point, we added each other online via the now-defunct chat program MSN Messenger, and spent the next few months talking/typing to each other about our lives. We started sitting next to each other in every lecture. We sent each other emails with our favourite music, drafts of our assignments and copies of our lecture notes. (Well, Evyn sent me his notes because I was always falling asleep in class.)

At the end of our first year at university, I invited Evyn to a concert where I'd be conducting a choir publicly for the first time. He turned up, watched attentively and made thoughtful comments. He smelled great. He had a *car*. A few days later, we snogged for two hours in the back of his Toyota Yaris hatchback. Shakespeare couldn't have written it. And now Evyn has been my best friend and calm support for seventeen years.

Evyn is astonishingly brilliant and infuriatingly humble in equal measure. He works extraordinarily hard. His study regime to prepare for his final radiology exams bordered on maniacal. So afraid of wasting a single minute, he kept reading his study notes through a watertight Ziploc sleeve while he showered. He was convinced he would fail. Of course, he received the top mark in the country.

We disagree plenty, but have never hurled a cruel insult or raised our voices at each other in anger. We are two independent, differentially anxious, strangely complementary people. We improvise songs for our dog, and watch movies, and listen to records, and we're so ecstatically happy to have found one another in this brief, precious life.

So, yes. I'm very proud of my relationship with Evyn. But to read aloud our – let's be honest – placid story in front of a live audience and Trent Dalton, whose book was on Oprah's best summer-reads list? No, thank you. I needed drama, mamma. If I'm gonna write an assignment, I want an A+. And I knew of a particularly fierce love story in my family archives, but I was only peripherally aware of the details. The time had come to delve deeper.

I needed to talk to my mum.

Some daughters talk to their mothers for hours every day. I don't understand it, but I'm happy for them. There's probably a mother and daughter out there right now, reading this book together on holidays, holding hands and turning each page as one. I think? I'm not really sure how it works. As a kid, I often visited Anglo-Australian friends' houses and looked on in confusion. Is that my friend sitting on her mum's *lap* while talking about her day? Not to mention, they greeted each other by kissing *on the mouth*! To me, being thirteen and mouth-kissing your mum 'hello' is the physical intimacy equivalent of headbutting yourself back inside your mum's womb for an afternoon nap.

Stranger still, five minutes later, my friend would be screaming 'I HATE YOU!' before slamming a bedroom door in a fit of tears.

JUNE

Her mum – the *adult* – would then apologise on the other side of the door. 'I'm so sorry, sweetie. You *can* pierce your bellybutton with a rusty nail. It's your body, your choice.'

Where am I? I wondered, as I quietly headed to their kitchen sink to wash some dishes, just in case this troubled family needed a reminder of how children were supposed to behave.

For my family and my fellow non-Western (mostly South-East Asian) friends, our main expressions of love growing up were acts of service and personal sacrifice. Not words and kisses, but work and outcomes. Even though my dad is white, my parents were a unified tiger parenting unit, who largely demonstrated their deep love for us by having really high standards and working endlessly to enable us to meet them. Dad taught at school all day, then chauffeured us kids to our infinite activities before returning home to cook and clean. Every day, my mum went to work at 5 am and came home at 9 pm (her actual work hours), and would take us to music lessons and cultural excursions on weekends. In return, we got As at school and practised the piano to show we were grateful. We also did this to avoid the racket of being disciplined. My siblings and I saved our emotional outpourings for our peers.

And I'm not trying to yuck anyone else's yum, but it is a fact that nobody in my family has ever mouth-kissed 'hello'.

My mum is a whole, complex person with a husband, a sister and friends of her own, and I am her stubbornly independent child with my own partner and social network.

We both implicitly understood and upheld this dynamic until this loveable bloke, Trent Dalton, asked me to tell him a love story. A few days before the event, I dropped by my parents' house with a bowl of fried rice (aka love) and asked Mum to tell me something deeply personal: the story of her mother. My popo.

Popo's love story is not a romance. It's a story of how love was breathed into existence. For some families, love is passed down generationally like wealth. In other families, love needs to be chosen and learned. And Popo did just that, even though nobody showed her how.

Through tears, words and not a single mouth-kiss, my mum poured out her soul to me.

'Mama's name was June, and she was born in 1919 as the fourth child born of a wealthy family in Kuching [in Borneo, Malaysia]. But she was their second girl – in a time and place where daughters were unwanted. Given the family already had the "burden" of one daughter—' My eyes connect briefly with Mum's and we both roll them in tandem. 'June's parents wanted to sell her.'

'*Sell* her! To whom, exactly?'

Mum tsked. 'I don't know, but the local priest heard of June's birth and made her parents promise not to sell her. So they did keep her, but she was never wanted. And all their subsequent daughters were discretely sold or murdered shortly after birth.'

'*MURDERED?!*' I gasped at the table.

Mum shrugged as if to say, *What can we do now?*

JUNE

She told me about June's childhood, which was filled with emotional and physical abuse. Never treated as equal to the rest of her siblings, June was separated from her family and forced to live and work like a servant.

June's eldest brother John felt sorry for his neglected sister, and looked for a way to free her from a life of cruelty. He reasoned with their parents that, if June was so unwanted, they should send her away to school. To do so would keep the promise they'd made to the priest, and the family could then be rid of her forever.

June was sent to a boarding school in Hong Kong. After fleeing the Japanese occupation, she eventually ended up in Singapore, where she studied further to become a nurse. It was there that she met my grandfather.

Sunny was a charming, handsome, charismatic businessman with the name to match. The son of a rubber planter in Malaya, Sunny was one of thirty-four children – born of three different wives, all of whom died during childbirth.

'So much easier than a man learning to use contraception,' I quipped.

Mum looked at me with disgust.

'Sorry! Sorry! I'm nervous hearing you tell me all this. Please keep going,' I said, cringe-smiling at my mum while thinking, *I've got to get a different personality.*

Mum forged on with her story.

'Except for two, all of Sunny's sisters were sold for money, while he and his brothers worked on the rubber plantation.

But when Malaya fell under Japanese occupation, Sunny was forced to work in a "Heiho".'

I nodded sympathetically to Mum, with my eyebrows knitted in concern like a good child who knows what a 'Heiho' is, while slyly googling the definition under the dinner table. FYI: they were groups of local youths who were forced to dig trenches and build fortifications for the Japanese occupiers.

In a brief, miraculous moment of opportunity, Sunny escaped the Heiho, but his troubles weren't over. He was then forcibly conscripted to work as a first aid assistant in Chumphon, where the Thai–Burma Railway was being built.

Some further, under-the-table research revealed that the Thai–Burma Railway is now more often referred to as 'the Death Railway project'. More than 100,000 people died during its creation. And 180,000 South-East Asian civilians were forced to contribute, of which Sunny was one. Unlike so many, he survived. Only just.

'How did he meet Popo?' I asked.

'She was his nurse in hospital,' said my mum.

Instead of interrupting, I raised my eyebrows as a visual exclamation point.

After World War II ended, Sunny and June were married in Singapore and had two daughters: my mum and my aunty Jacinta. But the marriage quickly soured.

'He was a terrible gambler, adulterer and liar,' my mum continued. 'We had a constant stream of debt collectors banging down the door of our housing estate flat,

JUNE

demanding payment. Mama told me that, when I was a baby, he signed me over as collateral for one of his gambling debts. She prayed every day for us to be free of him.'

My mum's voice was shaking with emotion. I scooped some more fried rice – which nobody was eating – onto her plate.

Desperate, June contacted her own estranged father for help. He remained true to form. June's father told her that he found her work as a nurse in leprosy clinics to be unclean and disgusting. That she was too useless to keep a husband. But that the greatest shame she had brought to the family was that she had birthed only daughters. He assured June that she and her two girls – his own granddaughters – would never receive support from him.

With a life where love was so often denied to her, June made a promise to her father, and to herself. She said, 'I will work every day to make sure my daughters do just as well in life as any sons. They will never be lesser because they are girls.'

And then, a bittersweet miracle.

A letter arrived in the mail with news from Hong Kong: June's eldest brother, John, who had fought for her to be educated, had unexpectedly died. An unmarried, single man, he had bequeathed a significant inheritance to June.

I felt some feeling of tension release in my brain. *'Finally.* A man behaves decently in this story.'

Mum nodded thoughtfully in agreement. 'I guess at that time, it *was* pretty extraordinary how he recognised that no woman could escape a cycle of abuse without the right resources.'

Quickly, quietly and methodically, June cleared any debts and bought a house independently from Sunny. She prepared for a life without him, and the moment presented itself.

'Mama returned from the hospital one afternoon to find him beating me with a rolled-up newspaper,' recalled my mum. 'He was thrashing me with all his might. Mama rushed in, put her body in front of mine, and told him to leave and never return.'

'And *did he?*' I asked with wonder.

'Eventually, yes. He went to live with his mistress. But *we* also left. Mama, Jacinta and I left the council flat without him, and moved into the home that belonged to us,' Mum says with a little upwards tilt of her chin. Sunny never crossed the threshold of June's home again. She poured everything into raising – alone – her two daughters.

My mum was crying hard now. I never see Mum cry. *Should I . . . offer her some more fried rice?*

'Mama sacrificed so much in life so we could have an education, which was the very thing that freed her from her own miserable life,' my mum said as she wiped her eyes and blew her nose on a paper towel.

June never strayed from her promise. She worked hard. Both her daughters went to university and pursued careers of service. One became a nun and the other – my mum – raised a family in Australia. June sent money to Australia.

JUNE

To *my* family. So her four grandsons and one granddaughter could have music lessons when their parents couldn't afford to pay for them.

And so love began with my Popo.

June was the reason my violin lessons were so important. She was my benefactor. *That's* why it was so crucial to Mum that I practise. To June, education was freedom. She wanted me to be free.

On June's final day in this world, her youngest daughter, my aunty Jacinta, attended her bedside.

'Mama,' said Jacinta, 'don't go home to God angry.'

June looked into her daughter's eyes, listening.

'Can you forgive your parents?'

June nodded. *Yes. Yes.*

'Can you forgive Dad?'

More nodding. *Yes. Yes.*

'You can go now, Mama,' Jacinta whispered.

June closed her eyes and died.

In telling this story to me, my mum said with amazement through tears of pride, 'I will never understand how Mama could love us so much, when nobody taught *her* how to love.'

But this tale tells me that love can begin at any time of our choosing. Because of June, my mum became a nurse. Then a midwife. She birthed her own five children: four boys and one girl. Then my mum studied law and worked as a solicitor. She became a barrister, defending Aboriginal and Torres Strait Islander children in court. Mum allowed me to tell this story to Trent. And gifted it here again for the final chapter of this book.

June believed in me before I existed.

June had four grandsons and one granddaughter.

I was never treated lesser because I was a girl.

I learned music because of June.

Thank you, Popo. I am free.

ACKNOWLEDGEMENTS

Thank you to anybody who has trusted me with their voice: in a singing lesson, a classroom, a rehearsal, a workshop or at Pub Choir. I think that every voice is a miracle. I'm humbled that so many people share their vocal magic with me. Please keep singing.

To Alex Adsett, who kindly harassed me for several years: you kept insisting that I was capable of writing a book and I'm so glad I believed you (eventually). Thank you for seeing something in me that I couldn't yet see.

Thank you to Emma Nolan from Simon & Schuster for trusting that I could do this. Along with Rosie and Jess, I'm so glad you supported me side-stepping anything preachy and self-help-y. Telling the truth felt great!

Thank you to Choirbolical, QKC, the Locks, the Worthingtons, the Shepherds, the Fletchers, the Mathiesons, Simon Turner, Gerald Gorman, Katherine Murphy and Dr James Cuskelly – I hope you know that your support changed my life.

To those who've shared their time and talents onstage, or backstage at Pub Choir, especially Waveney Yasso, Meg Bartholomew, Steve Thornely, Dana Gehrman, Sarah Koppen, Krystie McGregor, Mariel Hopper and Georgia Corowa: I am forever grateful our paths crossed.

To John Patterson, Paris Owen, Jacob Sosnowski, Jacob Morrison, Sahara Beck, Madison Rossetto and Sarah Wright: sorry I forgot to have a Christmas party in 2024, I was writing a book but I couldn't tell you about it. I love you all. Ha ha! Your boss said she loves you and she's also head of the HR department.

Thank you to David Law, Lily Bentley and Hugh Jorgensen: for being such important, treasured friends in my life but *also* for reading my first draft bilge. I trusted that you would help me and not judge me, and as always, you did both things in the exact right amount.

To my extended family, especially Yee Yee, June, Rose and all the women who've come before me: your shared courage is my intergenerational wealth.

To Timothy, Malcolm, Phillip, Hugh, Michelle, Wendy, Charlotte, Daniel, Vivienne, Ingrid and Magnus: I hope with this book I have advanced the name 'Jorgensen' for all. Please consider it 34 years of hugs and 'I Love You' from me, all at once. I am honoured to be the funniest person in our family.

To Mum and Dad: thank you for my life. I don't like to ponder on the specifics of that, but I am overjoyed to exist. Thank you for being the best examples of unselfish service I have ever known.

ACKNOWLEDGEMENTS

To Evyn: thank you. For reading every chapter, and singing every arrangement, and for loving me, and adoring me, and for wanting me to win *all the time*. You are the prize, FYI. I already won! Sorry for shitting in the shed.

ABOUT THE AUTHOR

Astrid Jorgensen OAM is a conductor, composer, entertainer – and now author – who believes that everybody can sing: not well, but literally. Founder and director of Pub Choir® and its online adaptation Couch Choir, Astrid is a global leader in communal, accessible music-making.

Armed with a razor-sharp wit and an unmatched enthusiasm for collaboration, Astrid has delivered her live, improvised comedy music lessons to hundreds of thousands of people worldwide. Her work has been praised by the likes of Marian Carey, Kate Bush, KISS, Radiohead and Sir Barry Gibb. Astrid's ability to enchant audiences and guide untrained singers to musical greatness has featured in international news outlets including *BBC World News*, *The New York Times*, *Vogue Magazine* and NPR as well as on TV shows including *Australian Story, Australia's Biggest Singalong, Spicks and Specks,* and *The Project.* In June 2025

ASTRID JORGENSEN

she wowed judge Simon Cowell when she appeared on *America's Got Talent*.

Under Astrid's leadership, Pub Choir has raised more than $550,000 for local grassroots charities – a number that continues to climb. In 2020, she was a finalist for Queensland Young Australian of the Year, and in 2024 received the Medal of the Order of Australia for her services to the community as a musical director.

Beyond Pub Choir, Astrid is a valued contributor to Australian television, radio and print media. She previously worked as a high-school music teacher, and her original choral works are frequently performed around the world.

Astrid lives in Brisbane with her partner Evyn, and a furious chihuahua called Penny.